Garden Wisdom

Garden Wisdom

SHARON AMOS

TRADITIONAL TIPS FOR MAKING YOUR GARDEN GROW

LAUREL
GLEN

This edition published in North American in 2000 by
Laurel Glen Publishing
An imprint of the Advantage Publishers Group
5880 Oberlin Drive, San Diego, CA 92121-4794
www.advantagebooksonline.com

Published in Great Britain in 2000 by Collins & Brown Limited, London House, Great Eastern
Wharf, Parkgate Road, London SW11 4NQ.

Library of Congress Cataloging-in-Publication Data available upon request.

ISBN 1-57145-665-1

Conceived, edited, and designed by Collins & Brown Limited

Editor: Gillian Haslam
Copy Editor: Alison Wormleighton
Designer: Christine Wood

Reproduction by Classic Scan Ltd, Singapore
Printed and bound by Dai Nippon Printing Co (Hong Kong) Ltd

This book was typeset using Berkeley and Berkeley Book.

1 2 3 4 5   00 01 02 03 04

Contents

Introduction   6

Earth   17

Air   57

Water   85

Plant Alchemy 105

Useful Addresses 124

Index 126

Picture Acknowledgments 128

Introduction

There is always something new to unearth about gardening—no matter how long you've been a gardener or how many gardens you've tended. You never stop learning: fellow gardeners, friends, and neighbors pass on hints and ideas, while snippets of useful information turn up in magazines and newspapers.

This book is packed with garden wisdom, and not just traditional tips and ideas, but some very new research, too. What links all the information gathered here is that every idea is simple, is easily achievable, and really does produce results.

The book is divided into four broad sections: earth, air, water, and plant alchemy. Earth begins at grassroots level, so to speak, and covers everything from newfangled ways of making compost to tips for aging terra cotta. It looks at how gardeners are taking a leaf out of the farmer's book and making more use of traditional green manures, and examines pest control techniques, both ancient and modern.

The section on Air deals with topics as varied as plants that thrive in shade, how to create an old-fashioned hot bed in a greenhouse, and how

best to store garden produce. It unveils simple ways to beat unseasonable frosts or, at the very least, minimize damage, and reminds us of country lore for predicting weather. It also highlights the wind's relatively unsung role in gardening, from wafting a flower's perfume abroad to attract pollinating insects to distributing seed far and wide.

Water considers ways of preserving what is fast becoming our most precious resource and how to use it effectively in the garden. There are tips for making a pond, and advice on both water-loving and drought-resistant plants.

Finally, Plant Alchemy begins with the art of companion planting—where one species appears to protect another against insect attack or disease. The scientific basis for many combinations is hard to verify, yet many gardeners find that growing French marigolds alongside their potatoes, for example, reduces the damage eelworms can do to the potatoes. This chapter also offers the opportunity for a nostalgic glimpse of the all-but-forgotten Victorian language of flowers, plus hints for deciphering Latin names—invaluable when deciding what to plant and where.

The Garden Shed

At its most functional, a shed is simply a tool house; at its most romantic, it is a private retreat. Of course, most sheds also have to double as places to store bikes and folding furniture and somewhere to keep the lawnmower under cover. They therefore tend to be a mixture of the two, catering to both storage and the need to escape, perhaps by leaving just enough space for an old chair.

Storing tools and vegetables

The easiest way to keep tools on hand is to hang them on pegs. This way, it's obvious at a glance what is in use or just plain missing. An old bookcase or set of shelves can hold small but essential pieces of equipment, such as garden twine, cane caps, scissors, plant labels, plant ties, as well as the inevitable old paint cans that tend to creep in.

If you have a greenhouse, it makes sense to set up a potting bench there where light is unlimited. If not, the only place for the bench is under the shed window, where you'll be able to see what you are doing. Just like a kitchen counter, the bench should be at a comfortable working height—around 3 feet high.

A corner of the shed can also double as vegetable storage. As it is likely to escape frost, you can safely hang up strings of onions and garlic, tuck away sacks of potatoes, and stack wooden trays of apples if you have room. Just keep an eye out for hungry mice and for any ill effects of dampness.

Good-looking sheds

It's not difficult to make a feature of a shed in the garden rather than let it be an unavoidable eyesore. Make a new shed fit in with the surrounding garden by copying some aspect of vernacular architecture. For example, if weatherboarding is used locally, paint the standard clapboard walls to match and re-roof the shed in the same materials as the house. Choosing a design with a proper pitched roof and casement windows can make all the difference, as it will help to tie in the shed with existing buildings. Boring creosoted pine can be transformed with attractive wood stains in shades of sage green, lavender, or azure blue, which in winter will add a welcome patch of color to the vista of bare soil and trees.

INSTANT INTEREST

Climbing plants soften stark outlines and veil a less than beautiful shed. By all means plant a rose or clematis, but while it is getting established, use rapid-growing annual species like the cup-and-saucer vine (Cobaea scandens) *with its curious flowers—it can grow 5 feet in a summer. Chilean glory vine* (Eccremocarpus scaber), *canary creeper* (Tropaeolum peregrinum), *and its cousin nasturtium are all useful for instant color and camouflage.*

A WOODEN BENCH PLACED IN A SUNNY SPOT OUTSIDE THE GARDEN SHED DOUBLES UP AS A USEFUL SHELF FOR CONTAINER-GROWN HERBS AND FLOWERS.

THE DESIGN OF MANY
GARDEN TOOLS HAS
HARDLY CHANGED FOR
CENTURIES. SIEVES, HOES,
BLANCHING POTS, AND
SHEARS ARE JUST AS
USEFUL TODAY AS WHEN
THEY WERE FIRST MADE.

Garden Tools

Gardening writers throughout the ages have been fond of compiling lists of essential tools. As long ago as the seventeenth century, spades, rakes, hoes, shovels, sieves, scythes and turf edgers, slashers, levelers, and tampers were deemed indispensable, along with scarecrows, water tanks, ladders, and forcing pots. By the time commercial catalogs were printed in the mid-nineteenth century, you could have been forgiven for thinking that it was impossible to grow anything without a battery of implements and an army of gardeners to wield them.

The bare minimum

The truth is that you can manage with as many or as few tools as you like, depending mostly on the size of your plot and what you are intending to grow. If you have a vegetable plot, then a spade, a fork, a shovel, and a hoe will be essential, along with a garden line to mark off rows, a dibble for planting out everything from beans to leek seedlings, and a wheelbarrow to cart manure wherever it is needed.

In a densely planted flower garden, it is possible to manage with a trowel, a small border fork, and a pair of secateurs (pruning shears). When the need arises, improvisation is the key—kitchen scissors cut sweet peas easily, while a garden fork can double as a rake.

Specialist tools suit particular situations. Anyone plagued by creeping buttercup will swear by a daisy grubber—a sort of fork with two prongs that slide either side of the offending weed so that a sharp tug pulls it out. If you have deciduous trees, a spring-tined rake is the best sort for teasing leaves out of borders, while a traditional besom makes light work of flicking them off the grass.

The invaluable pocketknife

Whatever else they may have hanging in the tool shed, most gardeners wouldn't be without a stout pocketknife. As well as its obvious uses for cutting vegetables like cabbage and lettuce, it can be used to trim leeks in the garden so that roots and leaves go straight on the compost heap. A knife can gouge out dandelions from a lawn and is ideal for weeding between paving stones and for marking out shallow seed drills.

Always buy the best tools you can afford. Stainless steel outlasts anything else, and provided it is properly cared for, a stainless steel spade will cleave through the heaviest clay soil. When you've finished working, clean off soil with a brush or a wedge-shaped piece of wood, then wash and dry the tools. Oiling metal from time to time keeps it in tip-top working condition. Don't neglect wooden handles either: keep them clean and, once a year, sand the wood lightly and rub in some boiled linseed oil.

CARE OF METAL TOOLS

To remove rust from the blades of secateurs (pruning shears), loppers, or any other metal tools, rub with a scouring pad dipped in lighter fluid. This is also useful to clean blades after pruning conifers with sticky resin or the sappy growth of shrubs. Wipe the blades with a soft cloth to finish and put the tools away in the tool shed—don't leave them lying around outside. A squirt of WD40 or similar spray lubricant will keep the spring mechanism working well. Some hardware stores and garden centers offer blade-sharpening services.

TRANSFORM A THRIFT-SHOP FIND WITH A SIMPLE
COAT OF PAINT FOR INSTANT GARDEN STYLE.

PAINTING FURNITURE

*Household enamel paint is fine for painting both wooden and
metal folding chairs, and it will last reasonably well if the
furniture is stored under cover in winter. For best results,
sand and prime surfaces first. Leftover latex paint can be
used to brighten up chairs and tables if you add a final
protective coat of varnish—nautical varnish is ideal.*

Garden Furniture

A garden is incomplete without somewhere to sit and admire the
fruits and flowers of your labor. Even if you are quite sure you will
never have time to sit on it, think of a bench instead as a focal point,
surrounded by shrubs or defined by an arrangement of pots.

Suitable seats

Matching form to the style of garden will make sure that furniture sits
comfortably in the landscape. Austere formal benches suit equally
formal gardens, laid out in well-defined beds or parterres and with
neatly clipped hedges. Cast-iron benches entwined with grapes, vine
leaves, and all manner of embellishments are of a more romantic
nature and sit better in a less restrained setting. In a truly rustic
cottage garden, homemade seats lashed together from hazel poles will
be at home, as will benches built from brick piers and old railway ties,
though creosote leaching out in hot sun can be a problem.

A comfortable perch in a retaining wall or terrace wall can be
created by laying a turf bench—for a scented version, use lawn
camomile or thyme—while old tree stumps make informal stools
about the garden. Some say the best way to appreciate a garden is
supine, reclining in a hammock, drink in hand. You can even buy
self-supporting hammocks that don't need to be fixed between trees.

Jazz up thrift-shop finds

Plastic really is best avoided: not only does it stand out starkly in a
garden, but it's also impractical. It ages badly, soon looking
unpleasantly dirty, and is very awkward to store, as typical sets of a
table and chairs do not fold flat. Although plastic furniture is cheap,
there are even better budget ways to put together a garden dining set.
For example, an old-fashioned card table with the cloth top stripped
off can be re-covered in oilcloth. Assorted folding chairs picked up at
yard sales and flea markets can be unified by a coat of paint.

DECKCHAIRS

....

The canvas "sling" of an old deckchair can become thin and worn, especially where it has rubbed against the wooden frame, but it's easy enough to replace. Pull out the upholstery tacks with a claw hammer and measure the length of the sling, then buy a replacement length of tough canvas from a fabric store or the fabric department of a department store. Nail it to the frame with new tacks. Modern deckchairs often come with detachable slings so that you change the chair's appearance to suit the occasion.

RIGHT: A COMFORTABLE METAL AND WOODEN-SLATTED CHAIR SET AT A PERFECT VANTAGE POINT, IN THE LEE OF A CREEPER-COVERED SHED.

EARTH

Soil

Soil is formed by centuries of frost, wind, and rain wearing away the bedrock of the land. Along with these minute rock particles, the decaying remains of plants and animals contribute to the soil's structure, which in turn is home to millions of microorganisms. Algae, bacteria, fungi, worms, and insects all make up a teeming community critical to the soil's health.

Sandy soil

Soil on sandstone bedrock is dry and light. If you pick up a handful and let it run through your fingers it feels gritty—sandy, in fact—indicating its free-draining nature. Sandy soil tends to run out of nutrients quickly, as they are leached away with rainwater. Adding plenty of compost or well-rotted manure is a good way to counterbalance this tendency. As well as providing nutrients, the organic matter bulks up the soil structure and slows down drainage.

Chalky soil

The topsoil on a chalk ridge tends to be shallow and often stony, studded with great flints. The soil is pale in color and free-draining; once again, lots of well-rotted manure is needed to improve water and nutrient retention. Chalk tends to be very alkaline, and organic matter adds acidity, creating a more workable balance. Where the soil is particularly shallow, it may be sensible to invest in some good-quality topsoil to build it up.

Clay soil

Clay is a heavy, sticky soil, waterlogged in winter and baked hard as a rock in summer. The same solution applies—add plenty of manure and compost—but in this case to open up the soil and improve drainage. The raw soil can seem intractable and digging can be disheartening work, but once several years of manuring and cultivating have passed, this becomes one of the best soils to grow on.

Gardeners who are fortunate enough to have a peaty soil or a rich alluvial silt deposited by an ancient river don't need to be reminded of it—they can just get on and grow things with very little effort. However, silt may need organic matter to assist drainage, while adding lime to acidic peat increases the range of plants that can be grown.

DIGGING CLAY

Because the sharp edges of a spade can actually flatten air pockets and make drainage worse, you should always use a fork to dig clay soil, in order to open it up. Where clay soil is very heavy and unimproved, try digging in gravel to a depth of around 1 foot. Always buy horticultural gravel from a garden center, as gravel from a builder's supply store may be contaminated with chemicals.

DIGGING IN WELL-ROTTED
MANURE IS THE KEY TO
IMPROVING MOST SOILS,
WHETHER YOU WANT TO
GROW PRIZE-WINNING
FLOWERS OR KEEP A
FAMILY FED THROUGHOUT
THE YEAR. SALSIFY,
PICTURED RIGHT, NEEDS TO
BE KEPT FREE OF WEEDS
AND WELL WATERED ALL
SUMMER: THEN IT WILL
REWARD YOU WITH LONG
WHITE ROOTS READY TO
DIG IN WINTER.

REMOVING LARGE STONES

On stony soil, dig up and remove as many large stones as you can. This is particularly important in the vegetable plot, where substantial stones and pieces of rock will affect the shape of root crops such as carrots, turnips, beets, parsnips, etc., causing them to become misshapen and twisted as they grow around the obstacle.

LIGHTLY FORKING OVER THE SURFACE OF THE SOIL IN THE VEGETABLE GARDEN CAN USEFULLY DISLODGE ANNUAL WEEDS. IT ALSO TURNS UP WEED SEEDS TO THE LIGHT SO THAT THEY GERMINATE. LET THEM SPRING UP AND THEN HOE THEM OFF BEFORE YOU SOW A NEW CROP.

Soil acidity

The fertility of soil is directly affected by how acidic or alkaline it is. When soil is too acidic, certain nutrients essential for growth become "locked" in the soil and thus unavailable to plants. Acid soils prevent plants from taking up calcium, and significantly reduce the amounts of nitrogen, phosphorus, and potassium they can absorb. Similarly, very alkaline soils lock up nitrogen, phosphorus, and potassium.

The level of acidity/alkalinity is indicated by a figure known as the pH value. For the best growing results, the soil needs to be neutral—somewhere between pH 6.5 and 7. It is relatively easy to adjust soil pH: digging well-rotted manure or garden compost, both of which are acidic, into alkaline soil can bring the pH down toward neutral. In the vast majority of cases, soil is too acidic and this can be corrected by adding slaked lime, which is alkaline, or spent mushroom compost, which usually contains lime. Adding lime to clay also improves drainage, because it causes minute soil particles to clump together—a chemical reaction known as flocculation—and this allows better movement of water, air, and plant roots through the soil.

Determining soil type

If you like gadgets, by all means use a proper soil-testing kit to determine your soil's pH, but you may not get an accurate overall picture, as pockets of soil can vary considerably. In fact, there is a much simpler method that gives a truer indication of soil acidity—it consists of just looking around at the plants that thrive in your garden and in your neighbors' plots.

Magnificent camellias, rhododendrons, and beds of heather point to the earth being acidic, as these species are all lime-hating. Where soil is predominantly alkaline, acanthus, lilac, clematis, and hawthorn are more likely to do well. Drought-resistant species such as broom (*Cytisus*), lavender, artemisia, and rosemary indicate sandy soil, which dries out quickly. Flourishing annuals smothered with flowers—for example, nasturtiums and species of lychnis—are a sign of poor soil depleted of nutrients. Plants that can tolerate heavy clay include roses, lilac, forsythia, and hellebores.

Preparing the Ground

The bare gardens of newly built houses, neglected vegetable patches, or gardens reclaimed from the grip of brambles are all sites likely to benefit from rototilling once the site has been cleared of weeds (see page 32). Rototillers—motorized, hand-held tools like mini-plows which turn the earth over—are readily available to hire from lawnmower and garden machinery specialists. By using one, you'll be able to turn over the soil much faster than by digging, though the machine can be quite hard to handle until you get used to it: you get the feeling it is going to run away with you.

Gardens on new building sites are likely to be severely compacted from heavy machinery, especially on clay soils. For best results, spread the cleared area with a layer of well-rotted manure first. The rototiller's blades will incorporate the manure throughout the soil and help distribute nutrients. If you've grown a green manure (see page 30), then rototilling it into the soil will help it to decompose faster by chopping it up and mixing in extra air.

There are some instances when a rototiller will make things worse. Never use one on soil infested with bindweed (*Convolvulus arvensis*), couch grass (*Elymus repens*), or dock (*Rumex obtusifolium*): chopping up the roots and distributing them through the soil will make these pernicious weeds almost impossible to eradicate, as each fragment of root is capable of regenerating. Another problem is that rototilling only works the top 6–8 inches, which can eventually cause the soil to compact below this level and prevent water draining away.

Digging

Rototilling is not therefore an alternative to digging—all land must be dug from time to time. A fork or spade used to full depth turns over around 1 foot and aerates the soil, improving drainage and making root penetration easier. When cultivating an area for the first time, it can be a good idea to loosen the subsoil below the spade's depth by working a garden fork to and fro.

Digging is essential on heavy clay, where it can help to break down clods into a workable soil. Dig clay in the late autumn or early winter and let the weather help, too. Exploit the action of frost on large lumps of soil: it breaks them down into smaller and smaller pieces as water penetrates cracks in the clods, then freezes and forces them apart. Breaking up surface lumps with a rake helps this process along still further.

ABOVE: THERE'S NO ESCAPING IT—DIGGING IS GOOD FOR THE SOIL AND IT'S GOOD EXERCISE, TOO.

RIGHT: A WHEELBARROW MAKES LIGHT WORK OF SHIFTING MANURE, GARDEN COMPOST, OR TOPSOIL WHEREVER IT'S NEEDED.

Raised beds for flowering plants

Where topsoil is particularly shallow, of poor quality, or composed of heavy clay, you can create a good growing environment with a series of raised beds. In the flower garden, these can be permanent structures built from pressure-treated timber, logs, bricks, or reclaimed railway ties, if you have the muscle necessary to maneuver them into place.

Even ugly concrete blocks make good retaining walls, and if you plant up the edges of the raised bed with trailing plants, they'll soon become invisible. But don't try to grow lime-hating plants in concrete beds unless you line the walls first with butyl rubber or tough plastic.

Fill the structures with either brought-in topsoil or soil from elsewhere in the garden—for example, if you dig out a path or patio—and mix in plenty of well-rotted manure or general garden compost. Raised beds are an ideal way to bring flowers and small shrubs onto a bare terrace.

Raised beds for vegetables

In a vegetable plot, raised beds don't have to be so pronounced— a height of 6 inches or so is sufficient. Neither do they need retaining walls, though if you want to use pressure-treated boards or railway ties here, there's no reason not to. The principle behind using raised beds to grow vegetables is to keep the beds small enough that you don't need to tread on the soil to work them. All cultivating and harvesting is done from the paths surrounding them, so for this reason they should be an absolute maximum of 4 feet wide. The soil structure stays light and airy as the beds aren't constantly trodden down, and raising the soil improves drainage and even helps the ground to warm up more quickly in spring.

The method also relies on planting crops closer together than on a conventional plot. Dense planting gives weeds much less chance to get established, reducing work on that score too.

You can create the beds as you do the autumn digging. Decide how long you want them to be and measure the land. Dig a trench about 2 feet wide across the bed to a spade's depth—a spit—and put all the soil into a wheelbarrow. Loosen the soil at the bottom of the trench with a fork and add a good layer of manure, then begin digging the next trench, using the soil to backfill into the first trench; the manure layer will raise the bed above the level of the soil. Continue in this way until you reach the last trench, which is filled with the soil from the wheelbarrow.

CUSTOMIZING SOIL

Use a raised bed to grow plants that otherwise wouldn't typically grow in your garden. Some of the most attractive plants that are fussy about soil type include camellias, rhododendrons, and azaleas. These species absolutely refuse to grow in alkaline soil, but raised beds enable you to control the growing medium. By starting off with a mixture of special lime-free potting soil and manure or garden compost—both of which are acidic—you should be able to maintain the ideal environment for these species. Annual top dressings of leaf mold, pine needles, or compost based on bracken or straw will help maintain acidity.

A VEGETABLE GARDEN THAT IS BOTH DECORATIVE AND PRODUCTIVE. SOME BEDS ARE RAISED AND EDGED WITH CHIVES; OTHERS ARE STANDARD BEDS MARKED OUT WITH LOW BOUNDARIES OF BOX. GROWING WITHIN THEIR CONFINES ARE CORN, RUNNER BEANS, AND HERBS OF EVERY DESCRIPTION.

Compost

Making good compost is rather like following a healthy diet: too many rich ingredients and the compost heap starts to look distinctly unhealthy. Mix in some plain, "high-fiber" elements and the end result is sweet-smelling, crumbly compost that is a pleasure to use.

Composting works by relying on soil organisms to break down plant material into a rich humus, just as they would naturally on the forest floor, in the hedgerow, and on grasslands. Worms, beetles, and woodlice burrowing through the heap leave behind digested material and useful air channels. Bacteria and fungi break components down further, generating heat as they do so, which speeds up the process still more.

What to include

Kitchen scraps make good compost. Keep a small tub by the sink and collect vegetable and fruit peelings, eggshells, used tea bags, and coffee grounds. Grass clippings and weeds can be composted, but to avoid distributing weeds along with the new compost, add only weeds pulled before they flower and set seed. (For pernicious weeds, see opposite.) New research has shown that newspaper, paper towels, and tissues can be composted, as can thin cardboard like cereal boxes and toilet paper tubes. Crumple newspaper so that it aerates the compost heap rather than smothering it.

The key to perfect compost is to keep a balanced mixture, as too much of one ingredient can turn the heap into a slimy, foul-smelling mess. Sloppy kitchen waste, grass cuttings, and sappy plant waste are the main culprits, so always counterbalance them with absorbent, fibrous paper or cardboard. Another good way to bulk up compost is to add old rags, but only from clothes made from natural fibers: cotton or wool, for example. Cut them into strips first to give them a head start.

ON THE VEGETABLE PLOT, GATHER UP ALL GARDEN WASTE IN A WHEELBARROW AND WHEEL IT STRAIGHT TO THE COMPOST HEAP. TRY TO TRIM FRESHLY PICKED OR DUG VEGETABLES BEFORE YOU TAKE THEM BACK TO THE HOUSE— YOU'LL ONLY HAVE TO BRING ALL THE TRIMMINGS BACK TO THE COMPOST HEAP AT A LATER DATE.

Dealing with Weeds

Tenacious weeds such as bindweed (Convolvulus arvensis), couch grass (Elymus repens), creeping buttercup (Ranunculus repens), and ground elder (Aegopodium podagraria) can survive the composting process, especially if the heap doesn't get hot enough. To be absolutely certain that these weeds won't continue to wreak havoc in the borders, tie them up in a black plastic sack and leave them out in the sun for several weeks before composting. Alternatively, leave them immersed in a bucket of water for a similar amount of time. You can use the leftover water as a liquid feed (see page 98).

What to leave out

Don't add meat, fish, bones, fats, oils, or cooked scraps to the compost bin, as these are likely to attract rats and flies. Instead, invest in a wormery (see below) to deal with them. Too many twigs and autumn leaves will slow down the rotting process or will be left unrotted in the finished compost, making it difficult to spread and use.

Compost heaps and containers

Composting can be as simple or as elaborate as you like. At its most basic you don't even need a container. Just start a heap on a patch of land that's not in use, using a base of twigs and branches to allow air to penetrate. Then one year later you can dig in the heap right where it's needed and cultivate that bed, meanwhile starting a new heap on a vacant bed.

In a small garden, a container will look neater. There are plenty of designs on the market, including cone-shaped bins, rotating drums designed to mix materials thoroughly, and wooden bins disguised to look like beehives. It is also easy to make your own compost bin by recycling old materials. An old galvanized garbage can makes a neat composter. Knock the bottom out, punch some holes in the sides to allow air to circulate, and dig it into the ground a little to keep it stable. A plastic garbage can is just as good if you saw the bottom off and make similar air holes in the sides.

A wooden bin can be made by lashing together four wooden pallets or by nailing scrap lumber to four posts firmly embedded in the earth. Using a pallet as a base for the heap improves air circulation, as does digging a cross-shaped trench and lining the sides so that they don't fall in.

Using a worm bin

There are plenty of wormery kits which come complete with inhabitants—brandling or tiger worms, which are the sort often used as bait by anglers. The bin has to be kept in a sheltered spot and ideally under cover in winter, as cold temperatures slow the worms right down. You can add meat, fish, fats, and cooked food scraps to the bin—all the ingredients you can't put straight on the compost heap—but you must feed the worms little and often. If you add too much food, it starts to decay before the worms have a chance to get to work on it. You can also add grass clippings and even wet newspaper from time to time. The resulting worm-cast fertilizer is rich in nutrients and micro-organisms and should be used sparingly as a mulch for plants in the flower border or as a between-row fertilizer in the vegetable plot.

TURNING OVER OLD LEAVES

Autumn leaves contain a tough protein called lignin, which is rotted down by fungi rather than bacteria, and the rotting process takes substantially longer than for other constituents of the compost heap. To avoid slowing the progress of the heap, make leaf mold separately. Sweep up the leaves and put them in black plastic garbage bags and tie the tops. Puncture the bags with a garden fork and tuck them away in a corner for a year if possible. Or make a bin from a cylinder of chicken wire and wooden stakes, and cover with a scrap of old carpet to stop the leaves from blowing around. Some leaves rot more slowly than others—plane and chestnut, for example, are two of the slowest.

LEFT AND RIGHT: RAKE
UP LEAVES AND GATHER
HANDFULS, BUT DON'T
ADD THEM TO THE
COMPOST HEAP—LET
THEM ROT DOWN
SEPARATELY (SEE ABOVE).
YOU MAY BE TEMPTED TO
LEAVE THEM ON THE
BORDERS TO ROT DOWN
NATURALLY, WHICH THEY
WILL DO, BUT AT THE RISK
OF HARBORING DISEASE
SPORES AND PESTS.

Manure

Introducing animal manure into soil adds nutrients and improves the soil's condition at the same time. Fresh manure can't be used directly, however, as it robs the soil of nitrogen when it rots down, starving plants of this vital nutrient and scorching leaves and roots. That's why the word manure hardly ever appears without the qualifying phrase "well-rotted."

The main source of manure these days is horse manure, which can be converted to a well-rotted state in about six weeks. It needs to be stacked into a heap and firmed down by treading or flattening with a spade to remove air pockets. Cover the heap with plastic sheeting, weighted down all the way around, and let nature do the rest.

If you are worried that manure may be contaminated with growth hormones, or straw bedding with herbicides and pesticides, the answer is to stack the manure and leave it for a year so that any residues can decompose.

Green manure

A green manure is a crop that is sown and then dug back into the soil when it has matured, returning extra vital nutrients to the earth while at the same time opening up a heavy soil or bulking out a light, sandy soil.

Although green manure is a centuries-old traditional farming method, it has only recently become popular in larger gardens. If you want to grow vegetables organically, it may be difficult to find a local farmer who can supply you with organic manure—and if they run a mixed farm, they'll need it themselves. A packet of seeds solves the problem quickly and simply and is a lot easier to handle than a trailer full of manure. Many green manure crops are leguminous plants that can take up useful amounts of nitrogen from the air, which is then added to the soil when the crop is dug in. They include various clovers, bitter lupins, winter tares, and trefoil, and can form a useful part of a crop rotation scheme (see page 34).

Prepackaged manures

Some agricultural waste products can be processed and neatly packaged and are useful for gardens where there is no room for a large, untidy stack of manure. Organic pelleted chicken manure is much easier to use than raw manure, though it's still quite smelly. Spent hops from the brewing industry are now available in pelleted form too: they improve the soil's moisture retention as they break down.

TREATING CHICKEN MANURE

Save the ash from a wood-burning stove or log fire and sprinkle it under the perches in the hen house. The ash dries out the droppings and reduces the smell. At the same time a chemical reaction takes place between the ash and the droppings, resulting in a better-balanced manure than untreated chicken manure, which is so strong and high in nitrogen that it should not be used on its own. The wood ash and chicken manure mixture can be used directly on the soil.

Mulching

Covering the soil with a mulch—a thick layer that excludes the light—is a good way of reclaiming neglected land. Keeping the mulch in place for a year will deal with the most pernicious weeds and disrupt the life cycle of some of the worst insect pests. Mulching on a smaller scale, in borders and vegetable beds, is an effective way to reduce water loss (see page 94) as well as to control weeds.

Putting old carpets to good use

To clear land effectively, scythe or rough-mow grass and weeds and rake them off the plot, then cover the area with the thickest, toughest old carpet you can find. Synthetic blends are best, as in extreme circumstances grass has been known to grow up through rotting wool-based carpets. To stop the carpets from blowing around, fix them to the ground with giant pins made by firmly hammering in bent wire coat-hangers. Put down the carpets in winter so that you have the whole year to make planting plans while the carpets put an end to couch grass and creeping buttercup. They will also trap plenty of emerging click beetles, whose larvae feed on plant roots and damage potatoes and carrots. Once land has been cleared in this way, it can be dug or rototilled and planted with potatoes to break up the soil still further.

Plastic sheeting

For the ultimate no-weed vegetable bed, black plastic sheeting comes into its own. The sheeting is spread over the whole bed, and plants of the chosen crop are dug into the soil below it via cross-shaped slits in the sheeting. The one drawback is that it is virtually impossible to water the bed. The best way to get round this problem is to lay a leaky hose—either proper permeable tubing or a perforated garden hose—under the sheeting and attach it to the mains as needed. To keep the sheeting in position, dig the edges into trenches all the way around the bed.

Strawberries grow well using this method and the sheeting protects the berries from mud splashes. Potatoes can be planted through the cross-slits, too, and won't need earthing up, as the black plastic excludes the light.

BLACK MAGIC

....

Black plastic sheeting is universally useful in the garden. Lay it on bare earth as a matter of course every winter and it will stop nutrients from leaching away, suppress annual weeds, and warm the soil up, which helps new plants get established and develop strong root systems. Roll it up and put it away when you start to plant, and it should last for several years.

Permanent mulches

If you plan to use a mulch as a permanent method of keeping weeds to a minimum in a flower border, you'll want to use something more attractive than plastic sheeting or old carpet. Shredded bark makes an effective mulch if spread to a depth of about 3 inches, but it is expensive. A budget alternative is to use black sheeting but disguise it with a thin layer of bark mulch. If you have a shredder, you can make your own by chipping tree and shrub prunings; although these are initially white in color, they soon dull to an acceptable brown.

SEAWEED MAKES A NUTRITIOUS MULCH, THOUGH IT IS RATHER SHORT-LIVED AS IT ROTS DOWN SO EASILY. ONLY GATHER SEAWEED THAT HAS BEEN WASHED UP ON THE BEACH, TO AVOID DISTURBING ROCK POOL AND SEASHORE HABITATS.

Crop Rotation

Crop rotation is a traditional growing system based on moving crops around the land, in order to reduce the build-up of pests and diseases in the soil and to avoid depleting the soil of nutrients.

Four-times table

The planting system is based on dividing vegetables into four groups: potatoes; peas and beans (legumes); the cabbage family (brassicas); and root crops. The vegetable plot is divided into four corresponding beds and each bed is planted with each crop in turn, on a four-yearly cycle. The crops have to be planted in a specific order for maximum benefit: one bed will be planted with potatoes in the first year, then with peas or beans in the second year, followed by cabbage of some type in the third year, and finally with a root vegetable.

Potatoes do best in well-manured acid soil, as this reduces the likelihood of their developing potato scab. For the next crop—peas and beans—the soil will need liming to bring the pH back to neutral. Peas and beans are nitrogen-fixers, so when they are finished, the top growth should be cleared but the roots left to enrich the soil with nitrogen. In the third stage of the rotation the cabbages will be protected to some extent against club root disease by the previous year's lime—which is thought to be even more effective against the disease if it has been in the soil for a year or so. Finally come root crops: carrots, turnips, parsnips, and onions.

Extending the scheme

If you have room, the rotation scheme can be extended to include a bed "resting" under a green manure (see page 30) and a strawberry bed. Some vegetables don't suffer from significant diseases and these can be slotted in wherever there is space. They include lettuce, squash, beets, and cucumbers. Don't forget to leave a bed for permanent crops like rhubarb, soft fruit, globe artichokes, and herbs.

(see page 30)

IN STRICT ROTATION

Potatoes cannot be planted straight after brassicas in crop rotation, as the lime that reduces club root disease in the cabbage family can promote potato scab. Always follow the strict rotation laid out on these pages to avoid this happening.

ALL MEMBERS OF THE CABBAGE FAMILY, FROM PURPLE SPROUTING BROCCOLI TO KALE, CAN BE AFFECTED BY CLUB ROOT, A FUNGUS THAT ATTACKS THE PLANTS' ROOTS. CROP ROTATION GOES SOME WAY TOWARD AVOIDING THIS.

Sowing Seed

There's a good reason for sowing seed in straight lines in the garden, even within an area intended to be an informal drift of flowers. Unless you are sowing a familiar species, the emerging seedlings can be difficult to distinguish from weeds, but by sowing in straight lines you'll know exactly which is which. In the border, once plants are full size, there will be no evidence that they were sown in such strict order. In the vegetable garden, regimented lines are what is wanted.

Sowing direct

Sowing seed directly into the soil where plants are wanted is the easiest method, especially for vegetables and hardy annuals. The soil should be raked first to break down any large lumps, then raked again to the proverbial fine tilth before seed drills—shallow furrows—are marked out, using nothing more high-tech than a stick.

For best results, sow seed thinly. Most commercially available seed has good rates of germination, and if seeds are sown too thickly, seedlings will compete early on for light and water. Fine seed is the hardest to control: one tried and tested method is to mix 1 ounce of seed with 1 cup of horticultural sand. Put the mixture in a bottle, insert a stopper made from a cork pierced with a drinking straw—formerly, a quill would have been used—then tip the bottle to sow the seed evenly.

To give seed sown direct a head start, warm up the ground by setting out cloches a couple of weeks before you plant the seed. Leave the cloches in place for protection and an extra-early crop.

Sowing indoors

For an even earlier crop, sow seeds indoors or in a heated greenhouse, where they can be kept at a high temperature. Heating cables and mats are ideal for directing heat where it's needed (see page 65). Seeds grown on a spare bedroom window sill grow strongly toward the light so need turning daily; they should also be moved into the center of the room at night, as the temperature close to the window falls dramatically. Never shut them between the curtains and the window, which is a recipe for certain failure.

A warm airing cupboard can be useful for germinating species that need high initial temperatures, but they need to be brought out the minute the seedlings emerge, as they will be weak and spindly if they spend time in the dark.

BEATING THE WEEDS

To reduce competition from weed seeds in an outdoor seedbed, prepare the bed a few weeks ahead and let the weeds germinate. Then hoe them off and sow seed immediately. The seedlings will have a head start before the next generation of weeds gets going.

Tough seeds

Some seeds have very hard outer coats: sweet peas and certain geraniums are renowned for it. Soaking them overnight before planting softens them and aids germination. If they haven't swollen in size, try "chipping" the seed coat with a knife at a point opposite the eye. Mice like to feast on sweet-pea seeds. Tradition has it that burying holly leaves in the trench alongside the seeds deters the mice from digging up the seeds and eating them.

Taking Cuttings

For the small amount of effort involved in taking cuttings, the reward is a garden stocked with favorite shrubs and flowers. Some species will take root with ease, just by pushing a pruning directly into the earth; others need a little more care and attention until they become established plants.

Easy shrubs

The tree mallow (*Lavatera arborea*) is one of the easiest shrubs to propagate from cuttings, which seem to root no matter what time of year it is, though the traditional time to make cuttings of deciduous shrubs is autumn. Similar easily rooted species include elder (*Sambucus*—*S. nigra* is useful for native hedging), forsythia, willow (*Salix*), philadelphus, and flowering currant (*Ribes*).

Cut stems about 10 inches long, strip off any remaining leaves, and cut off the growing tip just above a bud. Keep all cuttings where you can check their progress, in a prepared trench about 6 inches deep with a layer of sand laid in the bottom to improve drainage. If you don't have a large garden, a trench can easily be squeezed in at the back of a border, where it won't be too unsightly.

TAKE ADVANTAGE OF HONEYSUCKLE'S TENDENCY TO PUT OUT ROOTS WHEREVER A STEM TOUCHES THE SOIL AND CUT OUT ROOTED SECTIONS TO MAKE NEW PLANTS. CLEMATIS CUTTINGS ARE A LITTLE MORE TRICKY, BUT STILL WORTH DOING.

Propagating roses

Roses are surprisingly easy to propagate from cuttings, and the big advantage of roses grown on their own roots is that you don't have to worry about suckers from the grafted rootstock overwhelming the plant. The main reason that nurseries sell roses on grafted rootstocks is speed—they produce saleable plants a lot more quickly than cuttings. But since commercial considerations don't come into amateur gardening, rose cuttings are well worth taking. In autumn, take cuttings of stems that are about a year old, roughly the thickness of a pencil and about 6 inches long. Trim them back to a bud at each end, then just push them into the soil in a sheltered corner and wait. In a year's time they should be strong enough to transplant into their final growing positions.

Summer softwood cuttings

Fuchsias, abutilons, hydrangeas, and clematis can be increased by taking softwood cuttings. These can be started off simply by leaving them to root in a jar of water after the lower leaves have been removed. Or they can be potted into potting soil, four or five cuttings to a pot; the pot is then placed in a plastic bag, which is sealed to keep in moisture and warmth. Choose strong, healthy side-shoots without flowers for the best results.

DIVIDING IRISES

To increase stocks of irises that grow from rhizomes, such as bearded irises, lift clumps in midsummer every few years. Cut off the younger rhizomes from the edge with a sharp knife, leaving one or two leaf fans growing from each. Trim the fans of leaves right back so that the wind can't unsettle the replanted rhizomes. Discard the old, central section, and replant the rhizomes on the surface of the earth (with the tops exposed but soil around the roots)—for best flowering, they need to be baked by the sun in the summer. This method not only produces new plants but also improves the flowering potential of congested old clumps.

Pots and Seed Trays

Every gardener needs a range of plant pots, from the smallest size for starting off seedlings to large urns for creating displays around the garden. Nothing can beat terra-cotta for sheer good looks, but it does have some disadvantages. Terra-cotta is porous, which means the soil within dries out faster and plants need more frequent watering than their counterparts in plastic containers. Large pots are extremely heavy when planted, and, whatever their size, terra-cotta pots are easily broken.

Beware bad weather

Unless specifically sold as frostproof, terra-cotta pots can be vulnerable to damage in winter. Even a small crack will let in water, which expands as it freezes, forcing open the crack until the pot eventually breaks. Larger pots can gain a little protection with special clay "feet" that raise them off the ground.

If a pot does get damaged, you can still use it as a temporary container and plant it with summer annuals or bedding plants, whose roots are unlikely to exert sufficient pressure to break it open. Some hardware stores and artists' suppliers stock a special epoxy putty that can be used for minor repairs.

Even at the end of its life as a container, a broken terra-cotta pot is still useful. Put large broken pieces into a plastic carrier bag and smash them with a hammer into more manageable sizes, then recycle these as drainage crocks in the bottom of perfect pots.

The advantages of plastic

Terra cotta's porosity gives it a tendency to harbor plant diseases, whereas plastic pots are easy to sterilize: simply wash them in a very weak bleach solution and leave them to dry. Plastic pots are also very cheap to buy. For these reasons, professionals and anyone propagating quantities of plants usually prefer plastic pots. The same applies to seed trays. Traditional wooden seed trays look a lot nicer but are expensive and difficult to clean, and they do not drain as well as the modern plastic equivalent.

AGING TERRA COTTA

There are several tried and tested methods for ageing new terra cotta. Painting pots with yogurt or liquid manure encourages algae and moss growth but is slow to take effect. Rubbing new pots with parsley turns them instantly green, mimicking algal bloom, but the process is extremely tedious and tough on the fingers. Faking age with artist's pigment paints is quickest: mix different earthy tones with a water-resistant glue and sponge them onto your pots for instant antiquity.

Storing pots

Any terra-cotta pots that aren't permanently planted should be stored in a shed for the winter. Scrub them well and leave them to dry first. Small pots can be laid on their sides, tucked loosely inside each other, in a strong wooden tray. Never store pots in upright stacks, as changes in temperature and humidity can cause them to swell and stick tightly together, resulting in inevitable breakages as you try to pry them apart.

LEFT: PLANTS GROWN IN TERRA-COTTA POTS NEED PLENTY OF WATER IN SUMMER. IF OVERWINTERING HERBS IN POTS, THEY MAY NEED EXTRA PROTECTION: WRAPPING POTS IN BUBBLE WRAP HELPS TO INSULATE ROOTS.

BELOW: STORE POTS ON THEIR SIDES UNDER COVER IN WINTER. CRACKED POTS CAN BE HELD TOGETHER SUCCESSFULLY WITH A FRAMEWORK OF GALVANIZED WIRE.

Growing in Containers

No matter how much space you have in the garden, there are still plenty of reasons to grow plants in containers. Pots of flowers can be used to make a focal point beside a bench or doorway. They can disguise ugly pipework or gas meters, and can be easily moved into position to camouflage gaps in the border.

Choice of containers

As well as conventional plastic and terra-cotta pots, look out for household objects that have outgrown their usefulness but could be reinvented as planters. Old-fashioned tin baby-baths look wonderful massed with petunias, and clay chimney pots are ideal for trailing campanulas, verbenas, or petunias. Anyone who has spent a holiday in Greece can't fail to have noticed the empty cooking-oil drums—either painted or left boldly in their original state—that have been recycled to hold geraniums and lilies.

What any unconventional container must have is drainage: a hand drill can come in handy to pierce metal tins, while a nail heated in a gas flame should be sufficient to melt holes in plastic. Raising containers slightly off the ground on bricks, battens, or staging will help prevent drainage holes from becoming blocked.

What to plant

Containers offer a lot more scope for color and interest through seasonal planting—filling pots in summer with colorful annuals and replanting them with pansies or heather for winter color, underplanted with spring bulbs for the following season.

Permanent plantings tend to get rather neglected and tired-looking as the potting soil becomes exhausted of nutrients. Having said that, with proper attention, some shrubs can be grown permanently in containers and can actually benefit from having their roots restricted, promoting extra flowers in compensation. Species of rhododendrons, camellias, and pieris can all be pot-grown, so long as they are top-dressed with well-rotted manure in spring.

How to plant

Having chosen your pot, make a layer of drainage crocks at the base—the modern alternative to broken fragments of terra cotta is to recycle chunks of expanded polystyrene. Fill the container with a soil-based potting soil that won't dry out too quickly, and mix in some water-

CHIMNEY POTS

Instead of filling an old clay chimney pot with soil to use as a planter, find a container that fits snugly into the top of the chimney pot and plant this. Then you can simply lift it out to replant. If you want to shift the chimney pot, just remove the pot, lay the chimney pot on its side and roll it to wherever it's needed. This is a lot easier than trying to shift a chimney pot full of soil.

LEFT: SMALL CHIMNEY POTS OR
EVEN SECTIONS OF TERRA-COTTA
DRAINAGE PIPES MAKE IDEAL
PLANTERS AND ALLOW YOU TO
VARY THE HEIGHT IN A GROUP OF
POTS.

RIGHT: A PAINTED WINDOW-BOX
STYLE PLANTER IN SHADES THAT
ECHO THE SILVERY GREY FOLIAGE
OF LAVENDER, ROSEMARY, AND
SAGE. HERBS CAN BE GROWN AS A
PERMANENT CONTAINER PLANTING.

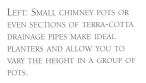

retaining granules, and a sprinkling of slow-release fertilizer. A combination of upright and trailing plants always looks interesting. Ideal trailing species include ivy, lobelia, helichrysum, some fuchsia species, and ivy-leaved geraniums.

Hanging baskets

Hanging baskets are notoriously vulnerable to drying out, so you must be rigorous about watering in hot weather. A good liner will help reduce water loss. Traditionally, wire baskets were lined with moss or foam, but you can now buy liners fabricated from recycled wool, from coconut fiber, and from cardboard, all of which come in unobtrusive earthy colors. In addition, an old saucer placed at the bottom of the liner before you add the soil will act as a shallow reservoir when you water the basket.

To be successful, hanging baskets need to look good from every angle—and that includes from underneath. To add plants all the way around the basket, carefully push their roots through the mesh or bars of the basket and through a corresponding slit made in the basket lining.

Window boxes

Well-maintained window boxes can transform the façade of a house but, conversely, nothing looks sadder than a few desiccated stalks in a neglected planter. Proportions are important, too: make or buy a window box that is the full length of the window sill—boxes that are too small look silly. Keep plantings low so that you don't obscure the light in the room and also so that you can open the window easily to water and feed flowers. The window box will need drainage holes in the base, and also a drainage layer. If the window box is heavy, fix it to the walls of the window recess with L-shaped galvanized brackets—you don't want to risk injuring visitors or passers-by.

STRAWBERRY PLANTERS

Tiered strawberry planters look pretty but aren't always effective because the lower plants tend to be starved of water and added food. To give every strawberry plant an equal chance, leave a section of drainpipe in the center of the planter when you add the compost. Fill the drainpipe with small stones or coarse gravel, then carefully pull out the pipe, leaving in place a central drainage core that will allow water to penetrate the depth of the planter.

LEFT: A CONTAINER OF GERANIUMS CAN BE STARTED OFF INDOORS IN A CONSERVATORY OR SITTING ROOM THEN MOVED OUTSIDE WHEN THERE'S NO LIKELIHOOD OF FROST. REGULAR DEADHEADING WILL KEEP GERANIUMS BLOOMING FOR MONTHS.

WEEDING PATHS IS A NEVER-ENDING
TASK AND ONE FOR WHICH MANY
PEOPLE ARE TEMPTED TO USE
WEEDKILLER. OTHER OPTIONS
INCLUDE WORKING ON YOUR HANDS
AND KNEES, CUTTING THEM OUT WITH
A KNIFE—ONLY VIABLE IF A PATH IS
SHORT—OR USING A GAS-POWERED
"FLAME THROWER." JUST A SHORT
BLAST HEATS PLANT CELLS TO
BURSTING POINT, THEN THE WEEDS
CAN BE LEFT TO DIE AND SWEPT UP
IN A FEW DAYS' TIME.

Weed Control

Before you plan a strategy for dealing with weeds, first ask yourself, what is a weed? All gardeners need their own personal definitions. In a wild garden or an informal cottage border, many so-called weeds that are actually wildflowers can look charming mixed in with cultivated species. Herb Robert (*Geranium robertianum*), for example, is a delicate cousin of hardy geraniums, with red-stemmed leaves and pretty pink flowers. Red campion (*Silene dioica*) is related to the showier annual lychnis species and is a welcome plant in shady spots; while statuesque teasels make ideal back-of-border plants. Late in the year, ivy is a valuable source of nectar for bees, and provides cover for roosting birds and nesting sites in spring. Don't be in a hurry to pull up nettles, either—they are a caterpillar food plant and also a lifeline for ladybugs (see page 113), which rely on nettle aphids as a food source early in the year.

Cunning weeds

Then there are weeds that try to fool you by looking pretty. Don't be weak and let creeping buttercup (*Ranunculus repens*) stay because its flowers contrast nicely with a purple hardy geranium: you'll regret it. More deceptively pretty thugs include ground ivy (*Glechoma hederacea*) and cinquefoil (*Potentilla reptans*)—pull them up on sight. Some weeds appear aggravatingly like proper plants: until it flowers, wood avens (*Geum urbanum*) looks just like rosettes of its cultivated relative geum, and it can take over a border in an instant.

Pernicious weeds

The hardest weeds to eradicate are bindweed (*Convolvulus arvensis*), ground elder (*Aegopodium podagraria*), couch grass (*Elymus repens*), and creeping thistle (*Cirsium arvense*). Where soil is infested with these, drastic measures may be necessary: a mulch of black plastic sheeting left for a year will smother most weeds (see page 32).

In the vegetable plot

When weeds are competing with crops for precious resources—light, water, and nutrients—you simply can't afford to be tolerant. Here, a hoe is the most useful tool, and the best time to use it is on a dry, windy or sunny day. Just pull the hoe through the top layer of soil and leave weeds on the surface to dry out and die. Hoe as often as you can: if you let weeds set seed, thousands more will germinate to take their place.

Weeds with long, fleshy taproots such as dock and spear thistles will grow again if you hoe the tops off, so these need to be dug out individually. If you have to leave soil uncultivated for any length of time, sowing a green manure will keep the weed population at bay, as well as benefiting the soil in other ways (see page 30).

GROUND ATTACK

Potatoes are an ideal crop for clearing soil of weeds. Their dense canopy soon shades out competitors, while their roots help enormously to break up heavy soil. Earthing up the rows turns over and uproots weeds, too. In a flower border use the same principle to suppress weeds by planting ground-cover species such as bugle (Ajuga reptans), sweet woodruff (Galium odoratum), low-growing comfrey (Symphytum grandiflorum), and some species of hardy geranium.

Pruning

Pruning can improve a plant's shape and appearance, encourage more flowers or fruit, and keep the size of shrubs and trees in check. Tools are crucial to pruning. Secateurs (pruning shears) are fine for use on woody shrubs but are generally designed to cope with fairly narrow stems—about ⅜ inch in diameter. For bigger stems, a pruning saw or long-handled pruners are more efficient. Blunt blades or inadequate tools will crush stems rather than slicing cleanly, making wood vulnerable to pests and infection.

Roses

Much of the pruning lore attached to roses is a legacy of the Victorian mania for producing prize blooms for exhibition, without too much thought for the appearance of the bush in the garden. All you really need to do is regularly remove the dead flower heads from repeat-flowering varieties, in order to keep a good flush of flowers going, and prune in spring in order to encourage vigorous growth, cutting back weak spindly shoots hardest of all. Although much has been written about where and how to prune, trials have shown little difference between roses pruned to a careful regime and those lightly sheared with hedge clippers.

Shrubs

The general rule when pruning shrubs is to note when the species flowers. Shrubs that flower after midsummer should be trimmed back in early spring, while spring-flowering shrubs are best pruned straight after they have flowered, to boost next year's blooms. If in doubt, refer to a handbook—there's nothing more frustrating than tidying up a hydrangea, say, and finding you've accidentally removed all the flowering stems for next year.

Buds always grow in the direction in which they are pointing, so for a balanced shape, trim above an outward-facing bud. Cutting too close to the bud risks damaging it, but, equally, leaving too long a stub causes unsightly dieback above it. By making the cut at an angle so that rainwater runs off, the stem is less likely either to rot or become infected.

Hedges

One of the most important considerations when pruning a hedge is to wait until the nesting season is over, to avoid disturbing garden birds. For a clipped formal boundary, trim bushes into a wedge shape, wider at the bottom than the top. This allows rain and sun to reach all parts of the hedge equally. Evergreen hedges must be well maintained from the very start, as you cannot cut into old wood—it simply won't regrow.

GRADUAL PRUNING

When restoring a neglected garden, don't be in too much of a hurry to hack back overgrown roses. Cutting an ancient rose right back in one go could prove such a shock to its system that the plant could die. Instead, exercise patience and cut it back by about one third of its growth each year to rejuvenate it with lots of healthy new shoots.

DON'T BE PUT OFF BY THE MYSTIQUE SURROUNDING ROSES AND HOW TO PRUNE THEM. JUST A QUICK TRIM IN SPRING SHOULD INVIGORATE MOST TYPES. DEADHEADING ENCOURAGES MORE FLOWERS IN REPEATING VARIETIES, BUT YOU MIGHT WANT TO EASE OFF TOWARD THE END OF THE SEASON IF YOU LIKE A DISPLAY OF ROSE HIPS.

Pest Control

It's surprising just how much you can do to control pests simply by removing them by hand, provided you do it as soon as you spot a problem and before it has time to get a hold. It's easy enough to rub off the first few greenfly on a rosebud, and cabbage white caterpillars—or better still, their eggs—are easily spotted on a leaf.

Many traditional remedies rely on luring pests away from crops or flowers so they can then be collected up and disposed of. For example, wireworms, which are the larvae of click beetles, make small holes in potatoes and carrots. Trap them by spearing chunks of old potatoes and carrots on sticks and burying them between rows of the crops. The stick acts as a marker so you can lift the traps and destroy them every now and then.

Slugs

Slugs are a near-universal garden problem. Methods of trapping them rely on their habit of hiding during the day: setting out grapefruit halves or slabs of wood and turning them over every morning usually reveals a fair number of slugs. If you can bear it, leave the traps upturned and wait for the birds to deal with them—or pick up the slugs and dispose of them as you think fit. They make a welcome snack for any nearby ducks or can be thrown into a pond for the fish to find.

Creating barriers is another traditional method used to deter slug attack. Rings of soot, crushed eggshells, pine needles, ash, and slaked lime sprinkled around vulnerable young plants are known to deter slugs with varying degrees of success. A more modern trick is to cut the bottom off a clear plastic drink bottle and use this as a mini-cloche to protect a small plant, but inspect the soil around the plant before you do so—there's nothing more galling than trapping a slug alongside a precious plantlet. These remedies apply to snails, too.

Moles

One tip for dealing with moles is to dig empty wine bottles into the soil near known runs—the wind blowing across the neck of the bottle is said to produce a sound that is unpleasant to mole ears. Traditional remedies include putting mothballs into mole tunnels and encouraging caper spurge (*Euphorbia lathyris*), which moles are thought to dislike, to grow in the garden. There is one consolation for molehills on the lawn: a molehill makes perfect potting soil for use in containers.

EARWIG TRAPS

Earwigs like to feast on the petals of chrysanthemums, dahlias, and clematis flowers, but you could try making an earwig trap to keep their numbers down. Traditionally this consisted of a sheep's hoof stuffed with hay and set on a cane among the plants, but these days it's easier to use an upturned flowerpot instead.

Earwigs will use the traps as shelters, so empty them regularly and dispose of the residents before they get a chance to dispose of your flowers.

SLUGS AND SNAILS ARE ALMOST UNSTOPPABLE AND ARE ONE REASON WHY IT MAKES SENSE TO GROW MORE VEGETABLES THAN YOU THINK YOU'RE GOING TO NEED. HERE THEY'VE EATEN A RUBY CHARD LEAF DOWN TO THE TOUGH MIDRIB.

Lawns

There's no getting away from it, lawns are the most labor-intensive area of the garden—that is, if you want a weed-free velvet sward rather than daisy-starred turf. Lawn mowers were invented in the 1830s; before then, the grass was scythed then rolled to smooth out any ragged patches where the turf had been torn up. Once the lawn mower was taken up with zeal by gardeners everywhere, mechanized leaf-sweepers, edging shears, and all manner of paraphernalia that is still familiar today soon followed.

Starting from scratch

The quickest way to create a lawn is to lay sod, but as these are expensive, sowing a lawn is still a good option if you have the time. The traditional time to sow is late summer, but early spring is a good second best. The ground needs to be dug shallowly, then firmed and raked to an even tilth before seed is scattered and raked in.

Fine-leaved *Festuca* and *Agrostis* species make a beautiful lawn but are not hard-wearing enough for family use; mixtures of ryegrass (*Lolium perenne*) and meadow grass (*Poa* spp.) are the toughest. For the most fragrant lawn try to get hold of seed for sweet vernal grass (*Anthoxanthum odoratum*) and mix some in—it contains coumarin for that characteristic new-mown hay smell.

Keep sparrows off a newly sown area by swathing it in horticultural fleece or, more traditionally, stringing it with black cotton, which deters birds from landing.

Planting bulbs in lawns

A lawn studded with spring flowers looks pretty at a time of year when the grass is not in use; they won't interfere with summer mowing as the flowers will be long spent by then. Snowdrops, crocuses, dwarf daffodils, and snakeshead fritillaries (*Fritillaria meleagris*) are all ideal candidates as they have low foliage that won't shade the grass. Plant them randomly by scattering them over your shoulder and planting where they fall, using a core planter to take out a cylinder of soil and turf which you then replace on top of the bulb. Don't mow the lawn until six weeks after bulbs have finished flowering, to allow time for them to build up food for next year.

Alternative lawns

Sweet-scented herbs such as thyme or camomile make alternatives to grass in small areas and are wonderfully aromatic when crushed underfoot. Both need a sunny site to flourish and camomile will need weeding from time to time, but neither needs mowing, just a clipping—preferably after flowering for a thyme lawn. For a camomile lawn, choose *Chamaemelum nobile* 'Treneague', which is a creeping variety that doesn't flower.

DEALING WITH DANDELIONS

To get rid of rosette-forming weeds on a lawn— dandelion, plantain, daisy—carefully tip a teaspoon of salt into the center of each cluster of leaves. This will kill the plant. If there aren't too many plants, just cut them out with a pocket knife and fill any resulting gap with a little potting soil.

TO KEEP A LAWN IN PEAK CONDITION, NEVER MOW IT TOO CLOSELY, WHICH RISKS CREATING BALD PATCHES QUICKLY COLONIZED BY MOSS AND WEEDS. SET THE BLADES TO LEAVE A SWARD OF AT LEAST ½ IN. DON'T THROW AWAY THE LAWN CUTTINGS—ADD THEM TO THE COMPOST HEAP.

The Cutting Garden

The traditional idea of having an area solely devoted to growing flowers for the house has once again become popular. By planting flowers for cutting, there's no need to agonize about robbing the borders of their finest blooms. A plot of just 10 x 15 feet will keep you supplied with enough flowers for yourself and plenty to give away to friends and neighbors. Even if you can't spare that amount of space, a row of china asters or dahlias squeezed in among the cabbages and beans will produce more than enough flowers to keep the dining table decorated throughout the summer.

Preparing and planting

While the ground should be cleared of weeds, it's not necessary to manure it heavily, as rich soil can produce lush growth at the expense of flowers. For spring bouquets, plant as many daffodils and tulips as you can cram in; you can safely ignore the recommended spacing distances as you are not making a permanent planting. Plant them in neat blocks, and criss-cross the cutting garden with plank paths so that you can reach the flowers easily when you need to cut them.

Cottage garden annuals are easy to raise from seed, and they make charming summer posies. Try clarkia, godetia, love-in-a-mist (*Nigella damascena*), cosmos, larkspur (*Consolida ambigua*), and sweet scabious (*Scabiosa atropurpurea*). For tall arrangements, grow hollyhocks, bells of Ireland (*Moluccella laevis*) with its curious green flowers, *Verbena bonariensis*, which has an open airy shape and small purple flowers, and the exotic-looking spider flower (*Cleome spinosa*), which is easily raised from seed.

Space permitting, plant a clump of perennial delphiniums, foxgloves, phlox, or verbascum in a corner of the garden, so that there's no need to deprive the borders of their stately spires.

When to cut

Always cut flowers in the early morning, when moisture and sugar content are high. Take a bucket of water with you into the garden and immerse the stems as soon as they are cut. When you are ready to arrange the flowers, recut them underwater to avoid getting an airlock in the stems that would slow down water uptake.

RIGHT: FLOWERS CUT FROM YOUR OWN GARDEN WILL BE MORE HIGHLY PRIZED THAN STORE-BOUGHT BOUQUETS. DELPHINIUMS, ANGELICA, PINKS, AND PHLOX ARE ALL PERENNIALS THAT CAN BE GROWN IN ROWS IN A CUTTING GARDEN.

BELOW: WITH THEIR INTENSE BLUE FLOWERS AND SILVER-WASHED LEAVES, GLOBE THISTLES (*ECHNOPS*) MAKE STUNNING CUT FLOWERS. THEY CAN ALSO BE DRIED FOR WINTER ARRANGEMENTS.

AIR

Predicting the Weather

Although the latest technology means that meteorologists are able to bring us detailed forecasts and long-range predictions, weather patterns still vary locally. By keeping a note of cold spells and by talking to nursery growers and other gardeners in your neighborhood, it's possible to build up a personalized weather map that will help you take the best possible advantage of the local climate.

Rain is on the way

Cloud formation is one of the most helpful indications in determining whether it's going to rain. Wispy cirrus clouds high in the sky generally mean good weather, while low banks of big, puffed-up cumulus can foretell a storm. It's a vast generalization, but if you bear in mind that, by and large, southerly winds bring rain, you can then make enough observations to get a more precise idea of which winds bring rain to your area.

Less reliable are folklore predictions of rain, which include cows lying down or huddling together and scented flowers smelling extra sweet when rain is in the air. Dandelion or daisy flowers may close up their petals, and clover and marigolds fold up their leaves, while the scarlet pimpernel (*Anagallis arvensis*) was once known as the poor man's barometer because of its tendency to open its petals in fair weather and close them when rain is due. Bees are said to stay in their hives when rain is imminent, while ants are sent into a scurry of extra activity. When a storm is due, birds may fall silent. If weather is getting worse on the coast, seabirds such as gulls may head inland, while species that soar on air currents in fine weather stay much closer to earth.

A cold snap

Unseasonable frost is one of a gardener's worst enemies. A cold, starry night, when there's no wind and no dew on the grass, is a pretty sure indication that the temperature is going to drop below freezing. Gardeners in the milder south should watch out for northerly winds bringing cold weather; in the north, clear weather following wind or rain can herald a sharp drop in temperature. For emergency measures to protect plants, see the following pages.

Snow is less of a problem since, once in place, it forms an insulating blanket across plants. It is often heralded by a curious gray tone to the sky from diffuse cirrus-type ice clouds, accompanied by a halo around the sun or moon.

FROST CAN BE BEAUTIFUL AS WELL AS TREACHEROUS, ETCHING WINTER STEMS AND SEEDHEADS WITH ICE CRYSTALS. DON'T BE IN TOO MUCH OF A HURRY TO TIDY UP THE GARDEN OR YOU WON'T HAVE THE CHANCE TO SEE EFFECTS LIKE THIS—AND THE DEAD MATERIAL OFFERS A DEGREE OF PROTECTION TO THE DORMANT PLANT BELOW.

Frost Protection

A frost in late spring can play havoc with spring-flowering shrubs, turning magnolia flowers an unsightly shade of brown and killing fruit-tree blossom before it has time to set fruit. It can also set back hardy annuals like sweet peas if they have put on a lot of fresh sappy growth. Early autumn frosts can catch you unawares before you've had time to put geraniums under glass for the winter or to pick the last tomatoes.

Preparing for late frosts

Late spring frosts can ruin a whole season of flowers, but if you know low temperatures are imminent, there are a few rescue operations. An old sheet thrown over a hydrangea bush or small magnolia will protect its flower buds—use clothespins to fasten it to twiggy branches. Use a cloth that reaches to the ground, as the object is to trap radiant heat from the earth and keep the temperature under the cloth above freezing point. Use the same principle to protect beds of smaller delicate species. Horticultural fleece is very efficient, but plastic sheeting or newspaper will do the trick—whichever you use, weight down the edges with bricks or stones.

Pear trees flower early and are particularly vulnerable to frost. Planning ahead is the best method, and planting pear trees—and plums, peaches, and apricots—on a southfacing wall goes a long way towards addressing the problem, as a south wall absorbs heat during the day and then releases it at night. If frost is predicted when the trees are in flower, cover them if possible with an old mesh curtain.

The roots of container-grown plants are vulnerable to freezing, and it is a sensible precaution to wrap pots in layers of sacking, newspaper, or bubble wrap. It may not look very attractive but neither does a dead plant. To protect the plant itself, make cones or teepees of newspaper stapled in place.

Heave ho

To stop a cycle of freezing, thawing, and refreezing heaving up the roots of newly planted shrubs, trees, and perennials, mulch frozen ground with straw, bracken, or prunings of evergreen trees. This way the soil stays at an even temperature, without expanding and contracting and forcing roots upwards. Fast thawing can have an adverse effect on the frozen buds of camellias, azaleas, philadelphus, and any spring-flowering shrub, so these species should be planted where they don't catch the early morning sun.

Homemade Mini-heaters

*To keep a cold greenhouse or conservatory
frost-free, make your own candle lamps.
Stand a candle in a terra-cotta pot, using a
layer of sand in the bottom for extra stability.
Then light the candle and invert a pot of the
same size over it, to form a safe mini-heater
that will take the chill off the air—you'll need
several to make a difference, perhaps more,
depending on the size of the greenhouse.*

USE CLOCHES TO CREATE A PROTECTIVE MICROCLIMATE FOR
TENDER PLANTS. ANTIQUE GLASS CLOCHES WERE
HANDBLOWN OR MADE LIKE METAL LANTERNS WITH GLASS
PANES. TODAY'S MODERN PLASTIC BELL CLOCHES ARE FAR
CHEAPER AND LESS EASILY BROKEN AND JUST AS EFFICIENT.

Windbreaks

Strong winds can scorch leaves and cause wilting through excessive transpiration—the process where water is lost from leaf surfaces. A windbreak can go a long way, quite literally, towards reducing these effects. A barrier 5 feet high, for example, can protect land to a depth of 100 feet in its lee. Adding a windbreak to a garden prolongs the growing season by a matter of weeks and leads to bigger crop yields and increased flowering in the resulting microclimate.

Slowing down

What's needed is something to slow the wind down rather than stop it. Solid walls or fences cause more problems than they prevent: when the wind hits the barrier it actually increases in speed as it rushes over the top and whirls and eddies on the theoretically sheltered side. A permeable barrier that filters and slows strong gusts will protect delicate plants more effectively.

A trellis makes a useful windbreak, provided it is strongly anchored. Using a green woodstain will make it less conspicuous, and climbing plants can be trained to grow up it for both ornamental effect and added shelter. Similarly, chain-link fencing makes a good windbreak and, though rather ugly on its own, is easily disguised with creepers and climbers.

Hedges are the best windbreaks but they do have drawbacks. They will compete for water and nutrients with the plants they shelter, and they can take up a great deal of room. Although a neatly clipped formal hedge does not take up a vast amount of space, an informal one can encroach into the garden by up to 6 feet.

PREVENTING FROST POCKETS

Creating a windbreak by planting a hedge or building a fence across sloping land can actually trap cold air in a garden and turn it into a frost pocket. To prevent this from happening, clear out the bottom of the hedge regularly so that air can flow in and out. Leave a gap at the base of a fence for a similar air flow.

On the vegetable plot

A hedge windbreak is less suitable for the vegetable plot, as it is too permanent. A temporary windbreak to protect vulnerable newly planted species need be nothing more than a length of netting fastened to garden canes. Even blackberries trained on a wire-and-post system will give some degree of shelter to plants alongside. A row of raspberries will have some effect, too, but blackberries are better as they hold onto their leaves longer. A line of Jerusalem artichokes makes an excellent windbreak in a vegetable garden and, although they can be invasive, there is one easy way to keep them under control—dig them up and eat them.

Greenhouses

In a cold climate, a greenhouse enables crops to be sown and harvested earlier than if they were grown outside, and it improves quality, too. Tomatoes and eggplant grown under glass produce better fruits than do plants exposed to the worst of the weather. Even a tiny greenhouse can be used to raise masses of plants from seed with a good success rate. Seedlings get far more light than those grown on the kitchen window sill and produce stronger, healthier plants that have a much better chance of survival when they are eventually planted outdoors.

Wood or metal?

A wooden-framed greenhouse will usually look better than an aluminum-framed version, particularly in a traditional garden setting, but will need more maintenance. Softwood greenhouses need painting regularly to stop the wood from rotting—creosoting the wood to preserve it is not an option as it produces fumes toxic to plants. Hardwood frames are far more weather-resistant but are, of course, more expensive.

Whether you choose a traditional rectangular greenhouse, a lantern shape, or a lean-to against the house, you must make sure your model has adequate ventilation to control temperature and humidity in summer, plus shading of some kind to prevent fierce sunlight from scorching plants. If the greenhouse has solid bases to the sides, then staging is vital to lift plants up into the light; it also makes a very useful surface to work at.

To heat or not?

A fully heated greenhouse will support exotic species, but at a price. For the average garden, cheaper options include simply keeping the greenhouse frost-free, by using a small paraffin heater or even a thermostatically controlled electric heater that kicks in when the temperature drops. A frost-free greenhouse is ideal for overwintering tender fuchsias and geraniums and for starting off the more unusual species of spring and summer bulbs. Rather than heat the air, electric cables can be laid to heat the soil in the beds, or in trays on the staging if you want to give seedlings a boost.

WATERING

GREENHOUSE PLANTS

Cold water can be a shock to plants in a warm environment, so keep an open tank of water in the greenhouse big enough to take a submerged watering can. Refill the tank every day and that way you can be sure that the water you use is at the same temperature as the greenhouse.

AN UNHEATED GREENHOUSE WILL ENABLE YOU TO OVERWINTER TENDER SPECIES SUCH AS GERANIUMS AND WILL GIVE SUMMER LILIES AND ANNUALS FOR HANGING BASKETS A HEAD START. IF YOU DECIDE TO HEAT YOUR GREENHOUSE, THEN YOU CAN TAKE YOUR PICK FROM A WHOLE JUNGLE OF TROPICAL SPECIES.

You're in charge

Plants in a greenhouse rely entirely on human intervention to provide water and food. About eight weeks after potting, greenhouse plants can run out of nutrients, as the soil is not part of a wider ecosystem where microbes and animals contribute to the cycle of decay and nutrient release. Regular watering can also leach goodness out of the potting soil. Liquid manures (see page 98) are the easiest way to feed plants in a confined space.

Making a hot bed

Traditional kitchen gardens that served great country houses of the past had elaborate hot beds for raising exotic fruits like pineapples and melons for the table. The same principle can be used in the greenhouse on a more modest scale to grow cucumbers, eggplant, and melons. To make a hot bed, you need fresh—not well-rotted, for once—strawy horse manure. Make a thick layer on the greenhouse border and cover it with a thin sprinkling of soil and a dusting of lime. Repeat the process two more times, then dig planting holes in the hot bed and fill them with potting soil. Add the plants of your choice and cover all with a final layer of soil. As the manure rots down it heats up and warms the plants gently—a great boon for slightly finicky crops.

Using a cold frame

A cold frame—a metal or wooden box with a sloping glass lid—is a useful adjunct to a greenhouse, to harden off pampered, glass-grown seedlings by gradually acclimatizing them to life outdoors. In small gardens, a cold frame can also be a greenhouse substitute, to grow early greens—radish, for example.

Spring cleaning

In an artificial environment, everything must be kept scrupulously clean, as pests and diseases can get out of control. Once a year, give the greenhouse a good spring clean. Empty it completely and tip out old potting soil onto garden borders. Wash pots and trays either in hot soapy water followed by a rinse in boiling water, or in a weak bleach solution. Clean the glass and scrub the glazing bars thoroughly. Scrub the staging in hot soapy water and rub the woodwork with linseed oil when dry. Greasebands, more usually sold to keep flightless codling moths from crawling up apple trees, will come in handy in the greenhouse—wrap them around staging legs to stop vine weevils from climbing up and laying their eggs in pots.

BIOLOGICAL WARFARE

Deal with greenhouse infestations of whitefly with the newest method—biological control. Various companies can supply parasitic wasps which are sent in egg form by mail order. Encarsia formosa lays its eggs in the bodies of whitefly, and the developing larvae kill off the host. Similar biological predators exist for other pests, including red spider mite, vine weevils, aphids, and scale insects. Biological control tends to work best in the enclosed environment of a greenhouse, where the insects are in close contact with their prey.

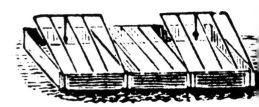

USE A GREENHOUSE TO GIVE PLANTS A GOOD START IN LIFE AND TO GET AHEAD ON THE GARDEN. IN A LARGE GREENHOUSE THERE WILL BE ROOM TO RAISE PLENTY OF SEEDLINGS FOR EVENTUAL PLANTING OUTSIDE, PLUS SPACE FOR CROPS SUCH AS TOMATOES, MELONS, CUCUMBERS, AND EGGPLANT TO BE GROWN ENTIRELY UNDER GLASS.

Scented Flowers

Flowers that fill the air with their perfume are merely enticing pollinating insects into the depths of their petals. The pleasure we get from inhaling their scent is incidental, yet a garden would be incomplete without fragrant flowers.

Roses

Roses have one of the sweetest scents, especially the old garden roses that flower for just a few short weeks each summer. In a setting where everything is expected to perform nearly all year round, gardeners may begrudge giving space to roses that bloom for such a short time, but true romantics never will. Blowsy full-blown cabbage roses (*Rosa* x *centifolia*) have the most intoxicating scent of all—'Fantin-Latour' is a perfect example with its many-petaled flowers in palest pink.

The best way to appreciate roses is to train a climbing variety or two over an arch that encloses a bench. 'Gloire de Dijon' and 'Zéphirine Drouhin' are two headily perfumed climbing roses that will soon embrace a simple arch, turning it into a fragrant bower in which to sit and dream. The vigorous rambling rose 'Albertine' has bright pink flowers that fade gracefully to blush pink as they age and a wonderfully fruity, lemony perfume.

Some roses even have scented foliage: the leaves of the incense rose (*Rosa primula*) smell sweet after rain, as do those of the sweet briar (*Rosa rubiginosa*), while the soft bristles that surround the flowers of moss roses can be attractively aromatic.

Evening scents

Roses are at their most intoxicating on a hot summer's day, but plants that depend on night-flying insects for pollination have the most intense scent from early evening onwards as the air cools. Night-scented stock (*Matthiola longipetala*) and flowering tobacco (*Nicotiana sylvestris*) fill a balmy evening with their fragrance and glimmer palely as color fades from the garden and dusk falls. The evening primrose (*Oenothera biennis*) is well known for powdering appreciative noses with yellow pollen, while the marvel of Peru (*Mirabilis jalapa*), with its pink-and-white flowers, is equally sweet-scented. Earlier in the year, the perfume of lilac flowers seems to intensify as the night draws on.

SWEET PEAS

To keep sweet peas flowering right through the summer, never let them set seed. As soon as seed pods begin to swell, the plant quite rightly feels its job is done and produces fewer and fewer flowers. At the same time, keep the plants well watered, especially in dry weather.

SWEET PEAS HAVE BEEN GROWN IN OUR GARDENS FOR MORE THAN 300 YEARS. MOST OF THE VARIETIES WE KNOW TODAY WERE DEVELOPED AT THE END OF THE NINETEENTH CENTURY.

Perfume underfoot

Planting a pathway with aromatic herbs makes walking around the garden doubly pleasant. Cushions of thyme spilling over from the border release a pungent scent when bruised by passing feet, while lemon verbena grows tall enough to be brushed and crushed with the hand as you pass. Marjoram, santolina, and sage make suitably fragrant edge-of-path plants, while rosemary and lavender bushes planted under the clothesline are a lovely way to perfume clothes and bed linen.

Garden seats are another prime site for perfumed plants. If you don't have a rose bower to sit in, you can make an equally fragrant spot by planting sweet rocket (*Hesperis matronalis*) and sweet mignonette (*Reseda lutea*) beside a bench. Sweet mignonette is nothing to look at— if anything, it is rather weed-like—but its perfume more than makes up for its appearance. Although it is a slightly tricky biennial to grow and slugs love the newly sprouted rosettes, it's well worth the effort. Growing lilies in pots that can be moved near garden seats or onto a terrace allows their beauty and fragrance to be fully appreciated as a succession of blooms wax and wane.

Scented geraniums are vastly underrated. Their elegantly shaped leaves release a surprising variety of scents when crushed. The best known is the lemon geranium, but their perfumes range from mint chocolate to orange, and from an aromatic resinous scent to a hint of rose like the fragrance of Turkish delight.

Spring and winter perfume

Many spring bulbs are scented but their fragrance is hard to appreciate until your nose approaches ground level. Snowdrops (*Galanthus spp.*), miniature iris (*Iris reticulata*), and primroses (*Primula vulgaris*) all smell sweetly but, at this time of year, scented shrubs are far more likely to be noticed. Winter honeysuckle (*Lonicera fragrantissima*) has tiny white flowers on bare stems; yellow spires of mahonia flowers smell like lily of the valley; and wintersweet (*Chimonanthus spp.*) has a pronounced honey scent. To best appreciate the fragrance of these flowers, place them in a spot that you visit frequently—for example, by the garden gate or the back door.

EARLY FRAGRANCE
....

Cut a stem of wintersweet (Chimonanthus spp.) *while the flowers are still in bud and bring it indoors for forcing. The warmth will induce it to bloom early and its honeyed scent will perfume a room for days. Try the same technique with mahonia, witch hazel* (Hamamelis spp.), *and clove-scented* Daphne mezereum *or* D. odora.

IT'S A CLICHÉ, BUT A PERFECT ONE. TRAINING HONEYSUCKLE ROUND A COTTAGE WINDOW AND UNDERPLANTING WITH ROSES—HERE 'CONSTANCE SPRY'—MEANS THAT THE MEREST BREEZE WILL WAFT SCENT INTO THE ROOM.

Seeds

Many seeds depend on a light breeze to distribute them—think of dandelion seeds with their delicate feathery parachutes, sycamore seeds that spin like helicopters, and great drifts of rosebay willowherb or thistle seed. That's why it makes sense to cut down or hoe up weeds before they flower and set seed—but similar properties in flowers can be used to a gardener's advantage.

Self-seeding

Letting plants self-seed saves a fair amount of work in the garden and a little expense too. If you don't like the position in which a plant has seeded itself, you can in most cases shift it somewhere more suitable, but some fortuitous, unplanned combinations can occur in this way. Plants to let have their head include forget-me-nots (*Myosotis*), love-in-a-mist (*Nigella damascena*), lychnis (*Lychnis coronaria*), foxgloves (*Digitalis purpurea*), sweet rocket (*Hesperis matronalis*), honesty (*Lunaria annua*), hellebores, aquilegias, and some campanulas. Once introduced into a garden, these prolific self-seeders are likely to stay if they find conditions to their liking.

Collecting seed

If you prefer to have more control over a plant's appearance, it is worth collecting seed and storing it for sowing the following year. It's best to leave seedheads to ripen on the plant and cut them just before the seed is released. In practice, this takes quite a bit of judgment and it can be easier to cut the whole stem, tie paper bags over the seedheads, and hang them up in a dry, airy room or shed. Never use plastic bags: they retain moisture and lead to rotting or mold developing, whereas paper bags allow plant material to dry out further.

Some species catapult their seeds far from the parent plant to improve their chances of survival. *Cleome spinosa*, sweet peas, and pansies should all have pods and capsules tied up in paper bags *before* cutting, in order to avoid triggering the catapult action and losing the seed.

You can collect seed from anything you like, but only seed from actual species or long-established cultivars will come "true," that is, resemble the parent plant. However, it can be quite exciting to sow collected delphinium seed, for example, and see what

ASSISTING SELF-SEEDERS

Give species that self-set seed, like foxgloves and forget-me-nots, a helping hand by shaking spent plants over the border before you compost them. You'll see foxglove seed in particular falling like a shower of finely ground pepper.

dazzling flowers it throws up. If you spot a strong, healthy specimen in the border that looks a good candidate for seed collection, mark the plant with a twist of colored yarn on its stem so that you don't forget it later.

Labeling and storing

Transfer collected seed into labeled envelopes to store. A sharply creased slip of paper makes an ideal "funnel" to tip seed from paper bag to final containers. The envelopes themselves then need to be stored in an airtight container—a tin if there is any danger of mice—and kept in a cool but frost-free shed or outhouse. If they come into contact with warmth or humidity, it can trigger germination or simply rot the seeds.

LEFT: WHITE FOXGLOVES ARE A NATURALLY OCCURRING FORM OF THE WILD FOXGLOVE (*DIGITALIS PURPUREA*), WHICH IS QUITE VARIABLE IN INTENSITY OF COLOR AND ALSO IN HEIGHT. LET FOXGLOVES SELF-SEED AND THEY WILL OFTEN COME UP IN JUST THE RIGHT PLACE, SUCH AS AMONGST THESE ROSES.

RIGHT: HELLEBORES SELF SEED FREELY UNDER IDEAL CONDITIONS AND THEIR SEEDHEADS STILL LOOK ATTRACTIVE IN THE BORDERS OR, AS HERE, AS CUT FLOWERS.

Plants for Sun and Shade

Growing plants in a sunny garden is easy: there's no need to give too much thought to what you can and cannot grow. Making a similar display in a shady garden, however, requires more planning and ingenuity. With a shady garden there are plants that you must forget about—to hanker after them is useless. In a sunny garden there are very few plants that will not grow, especially as it is easy to create a shady spot somewhere. There are disadvantages to a totally sunny site, though, such as the fact that you have to water plants more frequently. Also, if the garden is hot and dry, it may be too sunny for typical herbaceous sun lovers, and so you may have to restrict your planting to drought-tolerant species (see page 97). And when the sun is at its height, you need a shady place to sit out for summer lunches and teas—sitting in the full noonday sun is not only unpleasant but downright dangerous.

Sun lovers

Most of the great stalwarts of the herbaceous border need full sun to produce the best blooms. Delphiniums grown in a shady site, for example, will flower but the flower spikes will be sparsely scattered with individual florets instead of densely packed. Overall growth will be weak and spindly, too. It's implicit from their name that sunflowers must be grown in an open sunny site so that their huge heads can follow the sun's path across the sky.

Roses usually prefer a sunny garden and produce the most buds in full sun, though there are one or two climbing varieties that will tolerate a north wall.

The vegetable garden

There's no compromise between sun and shade when growing food crops. Vegetables, soft fruit, and tree fruits all depend on the sun to ripen them, and the vegetable plot should be sited in the sunniest part of the garden. Fruits such as peaches, nectarines, and apricots will positively benefit from being baked in the sun against a south-facing wall. Herbs, too, must have full sun to develop their intense aromatic oils and full flavor—their natural habitat is the dry sun-baked slopes of the Mediterranean.

ABOVE: SUNFLOWERS COME IN ALL SHAPES AND SIZES FROM VAST DISCS WITH A TINY FRINGE OF PETALS TO STEMS BEARING MULTIPLE SMALL BLOOMS. THEY NEED FULL SUN TO FLOURISH.

RIGHT: DELPHINIUMS AREN'T FUSSY ABOUT SOIL TYPE BUT THEY MUST HAVE SUN—THEY LANGUISH AND DWINDLE IN THE SHADE. THE VERY TALLEST SPECIMENS WILL NEED STAKING, ESPECIALLY ON WINDY SITES.

Gardening in shade

The most obvious option to adopt when planting in a shady site is to create a woodland garden. In this way you can take maximum advantage of early spring light when trees and shrubs are only just coming into leaf. Spring bulbs and tubers such as bluebells (*Hyacinthoides non-scripta*), snowdrops (*Galanthus spp.*), wood anemones (*Anemone nemorosa*), crocuses, and dog's-tooth violets (*Erythronium dens-canis*) will all flourish under the open canopy of trees and shrubs and sink back into obscurity as the shade thickens later in the year.

After spring, the picture gets a little more complicated. Much of a shady garden's interest has to come from foliage plants, with the odd splash of flower. Hardy geraniums have leaves in many different forms, from finely dissected to geometric; their flowers are pretty too, and some clumps can be encouraged into a second flush by cutting them right back to the ground after the first flowering.

Many species of hosta thrive in dappled shade and come in a great variety of foliage. Some leaves are a deep blue-gray, others are ribbed and reticulated, while yet more are splashed with white and gold. They will flower in shade, too, and some are sweetly scented. The worst aspect of growing hostas has to be the fact that they fall prey to slugs, and without some kind of pest control the leaves soon hang in tatters.

Dry shade

The worst possible gardening conundrum is dry shade. Thankfully, few gardens are completely dry and shady, but most have an awkward spot where precious few plants will grow—even weeds. The solution is to grow ferns, such as evergreen species of asplenium and *Polypodium vulgare*, which are at home in dry shade. Ferns will need a little help to get established, with copious watering and some well-rotted manure forked into the soil. But once they are strong enough, they can cope with the most unpromising situations and actually beautify them.

SHADY RAISED BEDS

Where soil in a shady garden is impoverished by greedy tree roots, make raised beds with lots of well-rotted manure worked in. In this way you can grow shade-tolerant lilies, like Lilium martagon, *toad lilies (*Tricyrtis*), plus hostas and traditional shade lovers such as lungwort (*Pulmonaria officinalis*), primroses (*Primula vulgaris*), and periwinkle (*Vinca major*).*

SHRUBS FOR DAPPLED SHADE

Hydrangeas are perfect shrubs for dappled shade—their native habitat is the edge of woodland in Japan. They bring color to a shady garden at a traditionally "dead" time of year—many species come into bloom in late summer and continue until the first frosts. There are three main flower types to choose from: classic mopheads; lace caps; and panicles, which have long loose flowers rather like sprays of lilac.

SNOWDROPS THRIVE IN SHADY GARDENS AS THEY ARE IN FLOWER LONG BEFORE DECIDUOUS TREES PUT OUT LEAVES. THEY LIKE WELL-DRAINED SOIL THAT IS NEVERTHELESS QUITE MOIST WHILE THEY ARE IN FLOWER. DIVIDE CONGESTED CLUMPS STRAIGHT AFTER FLOWERING, WHILE THE BULBS ARE STILL IN LEAF OR "IN THE GREEN." THIS IS THE BEST WAY TO BUY AND PLANT NEW BULBS, TOO.

Drying Flowers

Dried flowers are big business and store-bought arrangements are not cheap. By setting aside a row or two in the cutting garden or the vegetable plot, you can dry your own flowers and create year-round displays very easily.

What to grow

The easiest flowers to dry are those specifically grown for that purpose—the so-called "everlasting flowers" or "immortelles." Strawflowers (*Helichrysum bracteatum*) are like stiff-petalled daisies in hot shades of scarlet, gold, and yellow, and *Xeranthemum annuum* has purple, pink, or white flowers and attractive woolly leaves.

PRESSING FLOWERS

An old-fashioned flower press produces flattened dried flowers ideal for decorating handmade cards and papers. The presses often turn up in thrift shops and consist of two blocks of wood and four corner wing nuts that can be tightened to increase the pressure on the plant material. Layer flowers between sheets of blotting paper separated by corrugated cardboard and squares of newspaper to absorb all the moisture, and leave for several weeks, depending on the thickness of the flowers. Or simply press flowers between the pages of a heavy book; again use blotting paper to protect the pages.

CUT BELLS OF IRELAND, STATICE, AND HELICHRYSUM ON A DRY SUNNY DAY WHEN THE FLOWERS ARE AT THEIR PEAK. TIE THEM IN BUNDLES AND HANG THEM UP TO DRY FOR TWO TO THREE WEEKS, THEN THEY'LL BE READY TO ARRANGE.

Whether fresh or dried, gypsophila (baby's breath) is a useful flower for filling in spaces in any arrangement; its simple white flowers dry to small, round spheres. The familiar colorful statice (*Limonium*), also known as sea lavender, tolerates dry conditions and extreme heat —even salt spray—making it useful in the garden as well as for drying. Bells of Ireland (*Moluccella laevis*) is one of those curious oddities, a plant that appears to have green flowers, though these are, in fact, large bell-shaped calyxes that enclose tiny, almost insignificant, white true flowers. Once dried, they tend to lose their color after a while.

Ornamental grasses dry well. Look out for evocatively named quaking grass (*Briza spp.*), with its purplish-brown spikelets dangling from thin stalks; hare's tail grass (*Lagurus ovatus*), which has fluffy flower heads resembling, as its name suggests, hare's tails; and foxtail millet (*Setaria italica*), with its densely packed flower heads.

How to dry

All the species listed above can simply be cut and hung upside down in bunches in a warm dark cupboard or attic for two to three weeks. Some other garden flowers also respond successfully to this simple treatment, including larkspur (*Consolida*), love-in-a-mist (*Nigella damascena*), globe thistle (*Echinops*), and goldenrod (*Solidago spp.*).

Attractive seedheads can be cut straight from the garden and may not need further drying, but if they do, hang them in a large paper grocery bag or they'll scatter seed everywhere. Try love-in-a-mist with its horned, puffed-up seed cases; beautiful pepperpot-shaped poppy seedheads; and honesty (*Lunaria annua*) seed cases, which need to be stripped of their dull outer gray layers to reveal the silvery moons inside.

Using silica gel

Multi-petaled flower heads can be successfully dried in silica gel, a desiccating agent that extracts all the moisture from the petals. Use an airtight container and lay the stemless flower heads face up on a bed of the gel. Gently cover them with more silica gel and seal the container. The flowers will be ready when they feel brittle and papery (this can take anywhere from two to six days). Lift them out and shake off the excess gel, or use a paintbrush to flick it out from between petals. Use florists' wire to create stems for the flowers.

Storing Fruit and Vegetables

When faced with a glut of fruit or vegetables, the obvious solution today is to freeze the surplus, yet there are traditional methods of storing produce that are still well worth using. The key to keeping fruit and vegetables for any length of time is to start off with unblemished specimens that are also perfectly dry.

Storing apples and pears

To keep a supply of apples throughout the winter you need to start by growing late-ripening varieties. Pick them in late autumn or early winter when they are fully ripe. Use a cloth-lined basket to avoid bruising the apples as you gather them, then pick over the apples carefully and store only the best. Apples can be stored on trays, arranged so that the fruits don't touch each other, or wrapped individually in waxed paper to slow the spread of any mold or rot.

One old method advocates lining trays or crates with dried elderflowers before adding the apples. This is said to prolong storage and also to give the apples a distinctive hint of pineapple. A more modern method is to pack fruit in plastic bags, sealed with a twist tie but perforated with pinpricks so that the fruit can "breathe." Whichever method you choose, check regularly for rot or disease.

Pears tend not to store well, and even the latest varieties will keep for no more than two to three weeks on the shelf.

LEFT: CHECK APPLES REGULARLY FOR SIGNS OF DISEASE AND REMOVE ANY ROTTEN FRUIT BEFORE FUNGAL SPORES HAVE A CHANCE TO SPREAD.

BELOW: STORE APPLES BY VARIETY. THIS CUSTOM-MADE STORAGE BIN HAS SLIDING TRAYS WITH SLATTED BASES TO ALLOW AIR TO CIRCULATE.

Drying apples

There are various ways of drying apples, involving either heat or air. To dry them in a very slow oven—a warming oven is ideal—first peel and core the apples and soak them in salted water. Slice them thickly, then pat them dry before laying the slices on metal cake-cooling racks. In a conventional gas or electric oven, dry them on the lowest setting with the door ajar. Do this for three to four hours a day, for up to four days. When the slices are completely hard they should be left out in the air for a couple more days before being stored in an airtight container.

Alternatively, you can simply slice peeled and cored apples, thread the slices on string and hang the resulting necklaces above a radiator for up to a week. The slices will shrink but won't harden—they'll just feel leathery. Pack them in plastic bags, suck all the air out with a drinking straw, and finally seal the bags.

Storing vegetables

Savoy cabbages can stay in the ground all winter long but less robust varieties can be pulled and stored by hanging them upside down—root and stalk still attached—in a dry, frost-free shed, alongside strings of garlic and onions. They'll keep in this way for around two months.

Families need sackfuls of potatoes to last the winter months, and these are best stored in a frost-free shed. Use only permeable burlap or paper sacks and pack them with top-quality specimens. Every six weeks, carefully tip out the contents and sort through them, removing any potatoes that show signs of rot or deterioration.

Other root crops can be stored in old-fashioned peat boxes, though in these conservation-conscious times, it is better to use horticultural sand or vermiculite than peat. Carrots should have their tops cut off after pulling and then be laid on a bed of sand in a wooden box with no roots touching. Cover them with sand and add more layers until the box is full. Beets can be stored in exactly the same way, but leave about 2 inches of leaf stalk on the beets to avoid

OPPOSITE, BELOW: KEEP THE "STALK" OF DRIED LEAVES ON HARVESTED ONIONS—AND HEADS OF GARLIC—SO THAT THEY CAN BE STRUNG TOGETHER FOR STORAGE (SEE RIGHT).

BELOW: TOMATOES WON'T KEEP THROUGH THE WINTER. TURN THEM INTO CHUTNEYS AND PICKLES. GREEN TOMATOES PRODUCED TOO LATE IN THE SEASON TO RIPEN MAKE EXCELLENT CHUTNEY.

damaging them and causing them to "bleed." Rutabagas can generally be left in the ground without any ill effects, and parsnips are traditionally said to be much sweeter if pulled after the first frost.

Clamps and silos

If you have stacks of root crops to store, building an old-fashioned clamp could be the answer. Layer the roots in fine, dry soil in an out-of-the-way but well-drained site in a corner of the garden, then cover the resulting mound with a thick layer of straw—about 6 inches—followed by an equally thick layer of soil.

The same principle can be used to store vegetables in an underground version—a sort of silo. Dig a suitably sized hole and line it with bricks, then pack the vegetables inside between layers of sand, dry soil or even dry autumn leaves. Top with a heavy board to keep out mice, and dip into the store as needed throughout the winter months.

STRINGING ONIONS

To string up onions for storage, start with a length of string and a single onion. Double over the string and fasten to the onion stalk with a simple slip knot. Leave the onion hanging from the double strand of string and add more as follows. Take the next onion and, holding the stalk, thread the onion between the two strings. Wrap it around both strings and then bring it back through the middle of the two. Its own weight will help to keep the stalk in position. Build up the onion string by repeating the process.

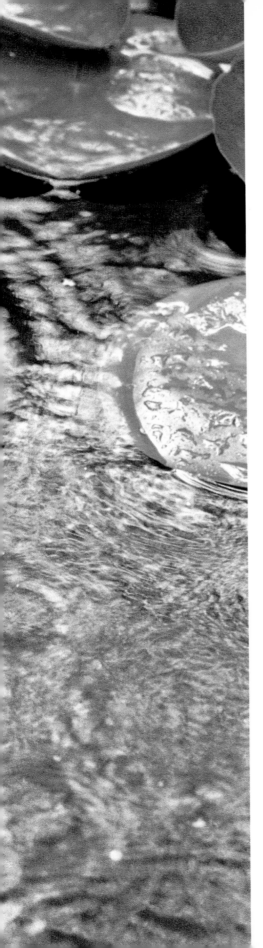

WATER

Collecting Water

Increasingly, water is valued as a precious resource, so it makes sense to collect, conserve, and recycle water in any way possible. A rain butt collects rainwater via the downspout that channels rain from the gutter into the drain or soakaway. With an average-sized roof, you should be able to install several butts at strategic points around the exterior of the house. Even a garage, shed, or greenhouse with a pitched roof yields a useful amount of rainwater.

Keeping a lid on a butt is important to stop small animals—not to mention children—from falling in. It also deters mosquitoes from breeding in the water (the larval stage in their life cycle takes place underwater). In addition, a lid prevents leaves and twigs from falling into the butt and clogging up the tap and your watering can. For the same reasons, it is worth making a homemade filter for the downpipe from a square of muslin or fine nylon—a pair of old pantyhose will do.

Recycling household water

Water butts can also be used to store domestic waste water that would otherwise go down the drain. Bath water is ideal, provided you keep soap and bubble bath to a minimum. If you have an upstairs bathroom, a diverter—a short length of pipe—is easily inserted into the bathroom waste-water pipe to transfer bath water to the water butt. It has the advantage of being detachable, so that you can remove it in winter when demand for water in the garden is minimal. For a downstairs bathroom, try siphoning off the water with a length of hose looped through the window.

The vast majority of water butts on sale these days are plastic, though in an unobtrusive shade of green. If you can't bear plastic, you may be able to buy a wooden version, but at a price. Whichever sort you have, raising the butt on a few layers of bricks makes it easier to fill watering cans from the tap at the base.

Watering cans

The plastic versus metal debate comes into consideration again when choosing a watering can. There's no doubt that plastic is lighter and easier to carry, but it doesn't age well and will split and crack when subjected to extremes of temperature. Galvanized metal, on the other hand, gains character as the years go by, becoming as treasured as a favorite pair of boots or a battered old hat.

Never leave metal watering cans outside in winter. Any rain that collects inside will freeze on a frosty night and the expanding ice will buckle the base, making the can wobbly and virtually unusable.

The most useful size of watering can is about 2 gallons. A watering can with a detachable rose is best—provided you are rigorous about returning it to the same shelf in the shed after use.

RIGHT: OLD GALVANIZED WATERING CANS AGE GRACEFULLY AND LAST FOR YEARS AND YEARS IF YOU PUT THEM AWAY FOR THE WINTER.

BELOW: A GREEN PLASTIC RAIN BARREL BLENDS IN TO THE BACKGROUND AGAINST A DARK FENCE AND A FEW PLANTED CONTAINERS NEARBY HELP SOFTEN ITS APPEARANCE.

LIME-FREE WATER

An extra benefit of collecting rainwater in hard-water areas is that it is ideal for watering lime-hating shrubs like camellias and rhododendrons. If you've gone to the trouble of growing them in pots in lime-free compost, you don't want to undo all your hard work when you water them.

Watering Plants

Few garden plants can survive without extra water to supplement rainfall, particularly at the height of summer. Watering is hard work, and to make sure it's not wasted effort there are a few rules to follow.

The best time of day

If possible, avoid watering in full sunshine on a hot day. Any water droplets that splash onto a plant's leaves will act as mini-magnifying glasses, focusing the sun's rays and scorching the leaves. Watering at the hottest time of the day also increases the humidity in the area immediately around the plant, producing ideal conditions for fungal spores of diseases such as powdery mildew and gray mold to germinate and multiply.

The cool of the evening has always been the traditional time to water plants, whether in the garden or in pots, as water is less likely to evaporate and has more chance of being taken up by roots. But recent studies have indicated that these very conditions, while benefiting plants, also encourage slugs and snails to come and browse, whereas seedlings watered at the beginning of the day suffer less damage. It's certainly worth experimenting with early-morning watering, even if it is only when plants are small and less able to withstand the onslaught of slugs and snails.

Watering techniques

When watering a plant, it is all too easy to wash away the surface soil and leave delicate roots exposed, especially if you are using a hose or a full watering can. When you are digging-in new plants, prepare in advance and reduce the risk of this happening, by firming the soil at the base of the plant into a shallow depression. When you water, this

SHOCK PREVENTION

Cold water straight from the tap can be a shock to a plant on a hot day. If you can't fill watering cans from a water butt, in which the water is at ambient temperature, fill them from the tap but leave them in the sun for several hours so that the water warms up.

FAR LEFT: RAIN DROPS ON A SCARLET-EDGED LEAF OF *THALIA DEALBATA*, A PLANT THAT THRIVES IN THE DAMP MARGINS OF A POND.

LEFT: EARLY MORNING DEW ON A PLUME POPPY LEAF (*MACLEAYA MICROCARPA*), A SPLENDID BACK-OF-THE-BORDER PLANT THAT CAN REACH 6FT.

"basin" will hold the water close to the plant, letting it seep down to the roots gradually and stopping any soil from being washed away.

It's always better to give a plant a thorough soaking just once a week rather than a quick sprinkling more frequently. Insufficient watering encourages roots to grow shallowly because the water doesn't penetrate to any great depth, and this causes the plant more stress as the roots are prone to being exposed or uprooted in strong wind. To direct water down to the roots of "thirsty" plants—tomatoes, for example—bury a plant pot up to its rim in the soil next to each plant when you set them out. Pouring water into the pot rather than the soil means it will go through the pot's drainage holes straight to where it's needed and won't wash soil away.

Getting rid of the competition

When water is scarce you can't afford to be lax about weeding, because weeds compete with plants for precious supplies. In a hot spell, the best method is to hoe the weeds off at ground level, severing the plants from the roots without digging them up. Turning over the soil to pull out the roots risks losing yet more water by exposing damp top soil. Fierce sun is usually sufficient to shrivel not only the weed but the exposed base of the stem, too.

Watering plants in pots

On a hot summer's day, when container-grown plants may need watering twice daily, the practicality of plastic pots can outweigh terra cotta's good looks. Plastic at least has the virtue of retaining some water, whereas moisture evaporates quickly from terra cotta. In a really hot spell, it may be worth shifting pots to a shadier spot to sit out the heatwave.

When planting containers earlier in the year, consider using water-retaining granules. A real scientific breakthrough, these long-chain polyacrylamides can hold many times their weight in water, which then becomes available to plants as the potting soil dries out. The granules can be either added to potting soil and watered thoroughly, or stirred in a bucket of water until they have swollen and then mixed into the soil.

Watering lawns

An established lawn should be tough enough to recover from lack of rain, but a newly sown or laid patch may need watering in its first year or two. A sprinkler is the easiest way to do it—move it around as each area becomes soaked. To make sure water penetrates to the grass on compacted soil, spike the lawn first with a garden fork to stop the water running off.

OLD-FASHIONED ENAMEL CANS, USED FOR CARRYING HOT WATER UPSTAIRS TO THE BEDROOM IN THE DAYS WHEN PLUMBING WAS STILL A RARITY, MAKE IDEAL GARDEN WATERING CANS.

Irrigation

While it may be galling to watch flowering perennials fail to thrive during a scorching summer, they may at least do better the following year. But in the vegetable garden you get only one chance for a good harvest, so it makes sense to plan some kind of standby irrigation system to compensate for lack of rain.

Lengths of plastic guttering, pierced at regular intervals and laid on the ground between rows of carrots, potatoes, or beans, will direct water far more efficiently than a watering can. Just empty the watering can at the top of the gutter and let gravity do the rest. It also means you won't be compacting the soil by trudging up and down between the rows. If you don't want to clutter up the vegetable patch with plastic, even a simple trench of similar dimensions to guttering will suffice.

Leaking pipes

Some manufacturers have produced irrigation systems based on porous piping, which can be either buried permanently in the soil or laid along the surface, and connected to an outside faucet when needed. You can make a somewhat crude version yourself by sabotaging an old garden hose and making small cuts along its length with a sharp knife. Lay the hose up and down the rows of vegetables and firmly plug the open end with a stopper, then turn the tap on carefully and slowly.

STORING A HOSE

Keeping a hose wound on a reel not only looks neater but evens out kinks and creases so that the water runs through properly without pressure spots building up. Some reels allow you to unwind just as much hose as you need, so that you don't risk damaging plants by hauling unwieldy lengths through the borders. Keep hose plus reel under cover in winter when not in regular use.

TAKING THE WATERS

The Victorians used water barrows to transport large volumes of water around the garden. These picturesque contraptions—rather like water butts on wheels—still turn up occasionally at architectural salvage yards or shops specializing in garden antiques, and are as useful now as they were when they were first made, especially if your vegetable plot is some distance from a tap or water butt. If you spot a water barrow for sale, snap it up immediately and put it to good use.

A SPRINKLER SYSTEM CAN BE THE ONLY THING THAT STANDS BETWEEN DESICCATION AND DROUGHT IN THE VEGETABLE GARDEN AT THE HEIGHT OF A HOT DRY SUMMER.

Capillary systems

Rudimentary irrigation systems can be useful in a greenhouse or for a collection of planted containers. To keep greenhouse plants watered, line plastic trays with capillary matting and stand groups of pots on top. Then use narrow strips of the capillary matting or lengths of twine or string (not nylon-based) to link the trays to a container of water: these will act as wicks and allow the plants to draw moisture from the matting and reservoir. This method is very useful for keeping houseplants happy while you are on vacation.

Mulching to Retain Moisture

A mulch—a layer of manure, compost, bark chippings, or other material used as a top dressing—not only improves soil and suppresses weeds (see page 32), but can also be used as a barrier to stop evaporation and keep the earth moist. Mulching for water conservation can only be done after a good downpour, however—anything less and you will simply *add* to the water problem, by preventing subsequent rainfall from penetrating the mulch and reaching the plants. By the same token, if you improve the water-retaining properties of the soil itself by manuring when you are preparing the earth (see page 30), you will be giving flower and vegetable beds a head start, which you can then build on by mulching.

How to apply a mulch

For a layer of well-rotted manure to be effective at reducing evaporation, it needs to be 2 to 3 in. deep. Leave a clear margin around each plant so that the mulch doesn't touch stem or leaves, which would cause them to rot. Eventually the mulch will be broken down by rain and by worm action, but it will at least last longer than if it had been forked into the soil.

Grass cuttings can make a useful mulch but they are tricky to use. If you spread them too thinly, they won't do the job properly, but if you layer them too thickly, so that the air is excluded, they may form an unpleasant-smelling slime.

Man-made mulches

Black plastic sheeting makes an inexpensive and effective barrier to water loss. Unlike manure, it is, of course, completely inert and doesn't condition the soil in any way. Its main drawback is that it needs to be securely weighted down if you don't want to find it wrapped around your neighbor's trees and bushes after a stormy night. Nor does it look particularly attractive. This is not necessarily an important consideration in the vegetable garden, but in a herbaceous border you would probably want to disguise it with a layer of soil or bark chippings.

If you don't want to face the eventual chore of digging up and disposing of the sheeting, experiment with a layer of newspaper instead. Try a layer of up to seven or eight sheets. Again, these will have to be weighted down but at least they will eventually decompose, though you may need to help them on their way by digging them in when they've served their purpose.

TO KEEP THE GRASS GREENER
....

During very dry spells, take the hood off the lawn mower and let the grass cuttings lie where they fall on the lawn. They will act as a mulch and help to keep the grass looking greener for longer.

ONCE PLANTS ARE IN FULL GROWTH IN THE BORDER, ANY UNSIGHTLY MULCHING MATERIALS WILL BE HIDDEN BUT STILL CONTINUE TO DO THEIR JOB. HERE A BARK-CHIPPED MULCH HAS BEEN EXTENDED OVER THE PATH.

A Good Start

....

Even tough, drought-resistant plants will
benefit from a little extra care while getting
established. It will also ensure that they
give their best performance later on.
Initially, protect small plants from wind
and extra-fierce sunshine—an upturned
flowerpot can be useful—and water them
until they develop a good root system. Once
they are growing strongly, they will shrug
off the worst the weather has to offer.

LEFT: LAVENDER IS A CLASSIC PLANT FOR HOT DRY
GARDENS, WITH ITS NARROW GRAY LEAVES AND
WOODY STEMS. ITS FLOWERS ARE A MAGNET FOR
BUTTERFLIES AND BEES.

RIGHT: *ALLIUM SPHAEROCEPHALON* LIKES A HOT SUNNY
SPOT WHERE IT WILL PRODUCE ITS DENSELY PACKED
HEADS OF FLOWERS IN MID TO LATE SUMMER.

Drought-resistant Plants

The way to avoid being a slave to the watering can in a sunny, exposed garden is to work with nature, rather than against it. Choosing plants suited to the conditions of the site can significantly reduce a gardener's workload. This is because plants that are native to hot, dry climates have evolved different characteristics to cope with the harsh environment. Species with silver leaves that reflect the light are far less prone to sun damage. Narrow-leaved plants don't wilt on a hot day because the leaves have a relatively small surface area, which reduces the rate at which they lose water. Succulent plants have their own reservoir locked in their thick, fleshy leaves.

Silver and gray plants

Jerusalem sage (*Phlomis fruticosa*) is a useful small shrub that thrives in dry sunny spots, and its soft gray leaves are complemented by flowers in a stylish shade of mustard. Various artemesias do well in similar situations and have fine, feathery, silver leaves that can be strongly aromatic. It is immediately obvious why perennial lamb's ears (*Stachys lanata*) can tolerate prolonged drought, as the thick down covering their leaves, which gives them their common name, protects them from water loss.

Narrow-leaved plants

Plants that survive on Mediterranean mountain slopes tend to be narrow-leaved species—spiky rosemary (*Rosmarinus spp.*), shrubby gray-leaved lavender (*Lavandula spp.*), broom (*Cytisus spp.*) with its diminutive leaves and tough stems, and pretty potentillas with their simple flowers.

Stiff, spiky phormiums can grow to quite a size and will tolerate windy seaside gardens, though they may need a protective layer of straw, bracken, or horticultural fleece to survive the winter. Their leaf tips can be very sharp, so position them with care in the garden.

Succulents

Succulent plants may look exotic, but there are plenty of hardy examples. Sedum is a classic cottage garden plant with flat flower heads that attract butterflies and bees, and its tough, fleshy leaves don't suffer in dry conditions. The houseleek (*Sempervivum*) can survive on little more than a tiny crevice in a roof tile, where it produces cascades of leaves arranged in rosettes.

Other affected sites

Drought conditions aren't confined to open, sunny sites. Most gardens have an area where water is scarce, which would be best planted with some of the species mentioned here. A border next to the house may receive next to no rainfall if the roof overhangs, and brick walls absorb moisture from the soil. Rain runs off or drains quickly from a sloping site, so plants there are vulnerable to drought, while strong winds are notorious for drying out soil and plants alike.

Liquid Fertilizers

It's tempting to imagine that by using a liquid fertilizer mixed with water you are doing two jobs in one—feeding and watering. But there are no shortcuts in plant care: if you use a liquid fertilizer when the soil is dry, you risk scorching the plants' roots.

Plants naturally take up nutrients in liquid form, so fertilizers dissolved in water are faster-acting than manure or powdered forms. They are ideal for correcting soil deficiencies and for supplying short-term nutrients. However, because they leach away into the soil, they are effective for a far shorter time than other fertilizers.

Making your own

Readymade liquid fertilizers are concentrated and convenient. Based on animal manure or on seaweed extracts, they should be diluted according to the manufacturer's instructions. But if you have the time and the inclination, it's very easy to make your own liquid manure. Just fill an old burlap sack about half full with well-rotted manure—any sort will do—and tie the top tightly. Then lower the sack into a large drum of water or even into a water butt, leaving a length of string showing so you can haul the sack out after two or three weeks when the water has turned as dark as mahogany (the sack will be very heavy by then so you may need assistance). Provided the soil isn't dry, you can use this liquid to water plants directly or you can dilute it with an equal amount of water and use it as a foliar feed.

Foliar feeds

Spraying leaves with a suitable feed has even more rapid results than watering with liquid fertilizer as the nutrients go right where they are needed and the roots mop up any spills. Early evening is the best time to spray leaves, when there's no risk of the sun scorching them. Foliar feeds are ideal for bulbs that have just finished flowering, especially those that are naturalized in grass, where there is competition for nutrients, or for bulbs in old, established clumps. Spray the leaves every two weeks or so, until they start to die back, and don't be tempted to cut them back or tie them up for at least six weeks.

HIGH-POTASH FEED

The perennial plant comfrey is rich in potash, an essential nutrient for flowering and fruit formation. To make a high-potash feed, fill an old plastic bowl with comfrey leaves and cover the leaves with water. Put a piece of old board across the bowl for a lid and leave for several weeks, stirring it from time to time. When the leaves have rotted, strain off the liquid and dilute it by ten parts of water to one of liquid before using it on the borders or vegetable patch. The leaf debris can go on the compost heap. This method also works well with nettles which you can gather from the hedgerows.

ABOVE: CARRY A BASKET OR PLASTIC BAG TO COLLECT NETTLES TO MAKE A HOMEMADE LIQUID FERTILIZER (SEE ABOVE), AND BE SURE TO WEAR GARDENING GLOVES.

RIGHT: WHEN BULBS HAVE FINISHED FLOWERING, SPRAY THEIR LEAVES WITH A LIQUID FERTILIZER TO BOOST NEXT YEAR'S BLOOMS.

Ponds

Not only are ponds stylishly ornamental—opening up a garden by mirroring the sky and creating a perfect spot for tranquil reflection—but they also encourage wildlife into the garden, with great benefits for plants and gardener. No garden is too small for a pond. Even a half barrel sunk to its rim in the soil, or simply placed on a patio, filled with water, and planted with water lilies, qualifies as an honorary pond or water feature, and it will still attract dragonflies and birds at the very least.

A larger pond will entice frogs and toads—both valuable allies in the war against slugs and snails—into the garden and they may even breed. It will also be a source of drinking water for small mammals like hedgehogs, similarly important consumers of slugs and snails.

Making a pond

The easiest way to make a pond is to buy a readymade shell, but if you prefer to design your own shape, then you'll need to line it with polyethylene or butyl rubber for maximum durability. Whatever shape you use, be sure to incorporate a shallow beach so that frogs and toads can scramble out easily and other animals can drink at the water's edge without the risk of falling in. To keep the water aerated so fish and wildlife survive, add vital submerged plants such as Canadian pondweed (*Elodea canadensis*) and *Potamogeton crispus*.

When you've excavated the area for your pond, rake it over carefully to turn up any sharp stones that may pierce the liner and cause it to leak. If the soil is very stony, spread a layer of sand over it, about 1 in. deep. For extra protection, you can buy special underlay from garden centers that specialize in aquatics—or try improvising with layers of newspaper or old carpet.

By extending the pond lining material well beyond the edge of the pond and under the soil, you can create an adjacent bog garden with permanently moist soil, though you may have to top off the pond more often, as water will tend to seep into the marshy margins you've created.

Positioning a pond

Ideally, a pond should be sited well away from deciduous trees and in a fairly sunny position. Autumn leaves rot down in water to produce methane, which will poison fish and other wildlife, while water plants can't photosynthesize in permanent shade and the pond will be colonized by undesirable algae in their stead.

WATER LILY LEAVES FLOAT ON THE SURFACE OF A POND, BUT IF THE PLANT BECOMES CONGESTED, THE LEAVES ACTUALLY GROW UP ABOVE THE SURFACE TO GAIN MORE SPACE.

Water-loving Plants

A pond in the garden or a patch of damp ground vastly increases the range of plants that can be grown. Of these, some species need to have their roots completely submerged in water while others prefer marshy or boggy conditions.

Plants for the water's edge

Plants that thrive right at the water's edge include arum lilies (*Zantesdeschia aethiopica*), yellow skunk cabbage (*Lysichiton americanus*), and the pickerel weed (*Pontederia cordata*) with its spires of blue summer flowers; these all love having their roots in the warm shallows. For a more natural look, add various native species like brooklime (*Veronica beccabunga*), figwort (*Scrophularia auriculata*), marsh marigolds (*Caltha palustris*), and wild irises (*Iris versicolor* and *I. pseudacorus*, blue and yellow respectively).

Deep-water plants

To plant the depths of a pond takes some skill and dexterity. Although deep-water plants like water lilies produce floating leaves and flowers, their roots must be firmly anchored. Start by planting water lilies in special perforated pots or baskets, lined with sacking or burlap to stop the soil from washing away—use specially prepared "aquatic soil" rather than economizing with garden soil, which can upset the nutrient balance of the pond. Add a layer of gravel to prevent the soil from floating out when you submerge the pot, then gently place the pot on the bottom of the pond. If the water is deep, lower the pot on a length of string.

Other species to plant in this way include water hawthorn (*Aponogeton distachyos*) and water violet (*Hottonia palustris*), plus marginal species like flag irises and rushes.

Bog plants

Plants that prefer the moist soil adjacent to a pond include several species of iris, candelabra primulas—native to damp Himalayan meadows—ligularias, and some ferns and grasses, but a surprising selection of border species also thrive under these conditions. Hostas, tall lobelias, phloxes, and buttercup-like globeflowers (*Trollius spp.*) all enjoy soil that doesn't dry out.

Planting a bog garden beside a pond simply involves bringing the liner up and over the edge of the pond and extending it under the soil for a distance (see page 100). You can use the same principle to make a bog garden alone, by digging out a bed to a depth of at least 12 in. and lining the base and sides with a sheet of tough polyethylene or butyl-rubber pond liner. Puncture the lining sparsely before replacing the soil so that some water can drain away and the bed won't become completely waterlogged and stagnant. Soak the soil thoroughly before planting. If you have children, this kind of garden is a safe alternative to a pond while they are young.

WATER LILY *NYMPHAEA* 'ESCARBOUCLE' HAS SCENTED FLOWERS THAT CAN BE AS LARGE AS 1 FOOT ACROSS. THEY PREFER DEEP WATER—AROUND 5 FEET IS IDEAL.

PREVENTING RAMPANT GROWTH

To keep vigorous species like skunk cabbage under control, restrict their root spread by confining them within plastic planting crates or similar containers improvised from whatever you have on hand.

PLANT
ALCHEMY

Companion Planting

Companion planting is one of the mysteries of gardening. It describes the relationship between two species, when growing them together actively benefits one—if not both—of the plants. It's an inexact science; what little research there has been into cause and effect is mostly inconclusive. Yet many gardeners swear by certain plant combinations, and companion planting is a method worth trying before you reach for a chemical spray.

In the vegetable plot

Various beneficial properties are attributed to French marigolds (*Tagetes patula*). Planting them between rows of potatoes can help limit eelworm damage to the potatoes, because the French marigolds' roots secrete thiophenes—substances that are thought to kill nematodes, particularly eelworms. The plants have the same effect when grown alongside tomatoes, which are also vulnerable to eelworms. French marigolds reduce whitefly attack, too, and alternating lines of the flowers with rows of cabbages seems to offer this vegetable some protection against brassica whitefly.

Culinary combinations can be effective as growing companions. For example, peppers (*Capsicum*) will suffer less from aphid attack if underplanted with basil. In addition, there is some evidence to suggest that peppers can themselves be useful companion plants. Their root secretions seem to protect plants such as runner beans and peas from a fungal disease called fusarium wilt, which also attacks sweet peas and dianthus.

Controlling caterpillars

Cabbage white caterpillars are the bane of brassicas, and there are numerous folk remedies for dealing with them. Interspersing rows of cabbages and cauliflower with aromatic herbs may help: sage, hyssop, rosemary, thyme, mint, and southernwood (*Artemisia abrotanum*) have all been recommended at various times in the past for deterring the female butterfly from laying eggs. Cropping cabbages with celery may also help.

SCENT WARFARE

There is a theory that the dreaded carrot fly finds its food plant by smell, and that masking the scent with a more pungent plant, such as onion, can make its task harder. Research suggests that you need at least two—and preferably four—rows of onions between each row of carrots for this method to be effective. There is also some evidence that the procedure prevents onion fly attack, making both plants joint beneficiaries.

RIGHT: TRY PLANTING ONIONS AND CARROTS CLOSE BY IN THE VEGETABLE PLOT (SEE DETAILS LEFT) AND YOU MAY BE ABLE TO CONFUSE TWO PESTS AT ONCE, BY MASKING THE SCENTS THE CARROT FLY AND ONION FLY USE TO TRACK THEIR HOST PLANTS.

BELOW: AROMATIC SAGE BUSHES MAY HELP TO DETER CATERPILLAR ATTACK IN THE VEGETABLE GARDEN. AT ANY RATE, YOU'LL HAVE PLENTY OF LEAVES FOR A CLASSIC SAGE AND ONION STUFFING.

Mutual friends

Other companion plants that actually benefit each other include asparagus and tomatoes. Planting tomatoes out in the asparagus bed after the last spears have been harvested reduces the number of weeds that will become established on the site and compete with the asparagus. Asparagus roots, for their part, appear to secrete substances that control the various soil pests affecting the tomatoes.

Gardeners have long recognized that potatoes and fava beans grown together produce better harvests than if grown in isolation—though, so far, no logical explanation has been found for this. Garden lore also recommends planting a clump of horseradish at each corner of the potato bed for an even better crop. If you try this method, be warned that horseradish is extremely invasive and will need digging up and reducing each year.

PEST CONTROL

Try alternating rows of cabbages and beans to deter both cabbage root fly and mealy cabbage aphid. The easiest way to grow them side by side is to choose dwarf beans and a fairly small cabbage variety.

UTILIZING NASTURTIUMS

If whitefly are a problem in the greenhouse, sow some nasturtium seed and let the plants scramble freely over the staging. They should make an appreciable difference to the size of the pest population. Nasturtiums can also help control aphids on broccoli and woolly aphis on apple trees. If the infestation is already well established, make a "tea" by infusing nasturtium leaves: cover them with water, bring to the boil, then take off the heat and leave to infuse for 15 minutes or so. Strain, cool, and dilute by a ratio of around one part nasturtium "tea" to four parts water before spraying affected plants.

LEFT: PERFECT TOMATOES DON'T ALWAYS TASTE THE BEST. THE ODD BLEMISH ON THE SKIN CANNOT DETRACT FROM THE SUPERB FLAVOR OF HOME-GROWN TOMATOES.

RIGHT: MIXING CROPS HELPS KEEP PEST LEVELS DOWN, EVEN IF YOU DON'T USE SPECIFIC COMPANION PLANTS—A LARGE AREA OF GROUND PLANTED SOLELY WITH ONE VEGETABLE POSITIVELY ENCOURAGES PEST POPULATIONS TO MULTIPLY.

In the flower border

Roses are extremely vulnerable to aphids, and tradition says that they are far less likely to be smothered with greenfly if they are underplanted with garlic. While mixing vegetables with flowers to this extent may sound a rather extreme solution, you don't have to take it too literally. Garlic is a member of the allium (onion) family, which includes a great range of ornamental species; underplanting with one of these should still have some effect. Mulching rose beds with onion and garlic leaves gathered from the vegetable plot is an alternative to making a permanent underplanting.

Other plants likely to benefit roses if grown close by include parsley, thyme, and catmint (*Nepeta spp.*). Catmint has traditionally been recommended for underplanting simply because its loose spires of flowers cover up any unsightly bare, prickly rose stems; however, it is now thought to have more to commend it than just pretty flowers. The poached-egg flower (*Limnanthes douglasii*) is often mentioned as a companion plant for roses, but this may be due to its attraction for beneficial insects like hoverflies, whose larvae prey on aphids (see page 112). Mignonette is a perfect sweet-scented companion plant but similarly may have gained this reputation for its insect appeal. Nitrogen-fixing plants such as lupins—whose roots contain bacteria that can increase soil levels of nitrogen, a nutrient vital for healthy plant growth—also seem to give roses a boost when planted nearby.

Some studies have suggested that azaleas and rhododendrons are almost guaranteed to thrive if planted with foxgloves, though the reasons are far from clear. But the idea gains support from a traditional method used to make cut flowers last longer: this involves making a "tea" from foxglove leaves steeped overnight in water, which is then strained and added to the flower vase. (When doing so, make sure that no one could mistake the concoction for a real drink: foxgloves are poisonous.)

Plants that repel other plants

If we are prepared to accept that some plants can benefit others, it seems a logical progression that there may be plants that can have a negative effect on neighboring species. Although the effects of companion planting are hard enough to quantify, those of allelopathy—the harmful effect of one species on another—are even more difficult to demonstrate. Plants compete naturally for light, water and soil nutrients, so these constraints have to be ruled out before it can be said with any degree of confidence that one species definitely has a detrimental effect on another.

A LEEK IN FLOWER (ABOVE) LOOKS POSITIVELY ORNAMENTAL, JUST LIKE ITS MORE SHOWY FLOWER-BORDER COUSIN *ALLIUM CHRISTOPHII* (ABOVE RIGHT). TRY UNDERPLANTING ROSES WITH ALLIUMS OF ANY DESCRIPTION TO CONTROL APHIDS.

OPPOSITE: FOXGLOVES SEEM TO HAVE AS YET UNEXPLAINED QUALITIES THAT BOOST GROWTH IN OTHER SPECIES AND CAN HELP CUT FLOWERS LAST APPRECIABLY LONGER IN WATER.

PLANTING ROSES

Never plant a new rose in a bed where roses have been growing as it will fail to thrive. This traditional piece of garden wisdom has been scientifically verified. Known as specific replant disease, it is caused by secretions from rose roots, which adversely affect newly planted specimens. Either leave the bed fallow for at least two years or replace the soil.

One fairly well-documented example is that of the walnut tree: rainwater falling on walnut leaves appears to wash off toxins, which then inhibit the growth of nearby plants. The tree's roots also seem to have an inhibitory effect on these plants. Similarly, adding pieces of walnut bark to tomatoes grown hydroponically makes them wilt.

Unexplained and largely unresearched garden examples of allelopathy include the fact that sunflowers and potatoes grown in close proximity appear to stunt each other's growth, while the two herbs basil and rue have an obvious antipathy and should be kept well apart in the herb garden.

Some flowers also behave badly when they are cut. Sweet peas, for example, give off minute quantities of ethylene—a gas that hastens ripening and decay, thereby causing other flowers to fade more quickly—and so should not be included in mixed arrangements. Mignonette, too, spoils other cut flowers in an arrangement, while lily of the valley and narcissus have a detrimental effect on each other if placed in a vase together.

Insect-attracting Plants

Insects have a vital part to play in the garden—their most obvious role is in pollination. Bees, wasps, and flies all fertilize flowers as they move from bloom to bloom in search of nectar and pollen: without this process no fruit and vegetables would be produced. For this reason alone, it is worth attracting them into the garden. But many species perform just as useful a service by devouring less welcome pests. Even wasps, which can be an irritation at the height of summer when you are having lunch in the garden, are useful to the gardener. They prey on cabbage white caterpillars, among other pests, so don't be in too much of a hurry to swat them.

Aphid eaters

Populations of greenfly, which ravage roses, and blackfly, which decimate fava beans, can be significantly reduced by encouraging predatory insects to feed on them. Hoverfly larvae are voracious consumers of aphids—a single larva will have eaten up to 600 before it metamorphoses into an adult fly. To build up the hoverfly population you need to start by attracting adults, which feed on nectar and pollen. Unlike, say, bees, hoverflies do not have long probosces, so they can only feed from simple, open flowers. Members of the umbellifer family are ideal. These are plants with flat, open heads composed of hundreds of tiny flowers. They include angelica (*Angelica archangelica*), yarrow (*Achillea millefolium*), cow parsley (*Anthriscus sylvestris*), dill (*Anethum graveolens*), and fennel (*Foeniculum vulgare*). Fennel is extraordinarily popular with insects of all kinds. Experiments have recorded nearly 500 different species that feed on its flowers, including tiny parasitic wasps whose larvae feed on aphids and caterpillars.

Research has shown that hoverflies are particularly attracted to the poached-egg flower (*Limnanthes douglasii*), which has simple open flowers rich in nectar. By sowing them between rows of fava beans,

EXTENDING THE FLOWERING SEASON

*Keep the beneficial insect population at full strength by extending your garden's flowering season at either end of the year. Hazel and willow catkins are an early source of nectar, while Michaelmas daisies are nectar-rich autumn plants, superseded by ivy flowers in winter. To boost supplies at the height of summer, plant eryngium, Californian poppies (*Eschscholzia californica*), candytuft (*Iberis*), fennel, angelica, Shasta daisies (*Leucanthemum x superbum*), convolvulus (*Convolvulus tricolor*), phacelia, and annual sunflowers.*

you can draw the hoverflies right in where they are needed. Females will then lay eggs in the aphid colonies so that the larvae have a readymade food supply when they hatch. The poached-egg flower has the extra advantage of being a bee plant, attracting both pest predators and pollinators in one go.

Ladybug, ladybug

Adult ladybugs and their larvae both feed on aphids. Early in the year when the first ladybugs are abroad, aphids can be scarce. But one of the first plants to become infested with aphids is the nettle. By leaving a patch of nettles in a corner you can provide a vital early food source for ladybugs. Later on, when the garden is in full bloom, cutting down the nettles ensures that they move on to help out on other garden plants.

Adult ladybugs overwinter in hollow stems, so it doesn't pay to be too tidy in the garden. Resisting the temptation to chop down spent hollyhock stems could make all the difference to your ladybug population.

BELOW RIGHT: CATKINS ARE A VITAL SOURCE OF NECTAR FOR BEES AND OTHER BENEFICIAL INSECTS WHEN FLOWERING PLANTS ARE THIN ON THE GROUND.

BELOW: EVEN IF YOU ARE SKEPTICAL ABOUT COMPANION PLANTING, MIXING FLOWERING PLANTS WITH CROPS SUCH AS TOMATOES ATTRACTS USEFUL POLLINATING INSECTS.

Plants that Repel Insects

While there are beneficial insects to be encouraged in the garden, the same cannot be said of insects indoors. Rather than resorting to chemical sprays and powders, it is worth trying some traditional remedies utilizing plants.

Deterring flies and other kitchen pests

One country custom to keep flies out of the kitchen is to hang up a large bunch of mint, though it is best to do this before it flowers—or to cut the flower spikes off—as flies are frequent visitors to mint flowers in the herb garden.

Elder leaves are thought to have similar fly-repelling properties and are said to deter wasps, too. In the past, swatches of elder were laid across baskets of soft fruits on their way to market, and strawberry and raspberry containers were edged with twists of the leaves. For obvious reasons, elder bushes were often left to flourish alongside outdoor privies—alongside sweetly scented jasmine—or deliberately set under the windows of farm dairies.

The pungent leaves and flowers of African and French marigolds (*Tagetes*) are said to repel houseflies, so a jelly jar of these flowers on an open window sill may warn off unwelcome insect invaders. Sprigs of fresh tansy can also be effective fly repellents.

The worst kitchen intruders are cockroaches, but one folk remedy suggests that cockroaches dislike the scent of bay leaves, which should be liberally scattered on kitchen shelves and in cupboards. To deter ants, sprinkle shelves with pennyroyal (*Mentha pulegium*).

Moth (and mouse) repellents

Elsewhere around the house, clothes moths can be a problem, particularly when woollen fabrics are folded away for the summer and likewise silks and linens during winter. Tried-and-tested moth repellents include dried lavender, sown into traditional cotton bags to avoid scattering loose flowers everywhere. In colder areas, where lavender is hard to grow, dried thyme was sometimes used as a substitute. Lavender's repellent properties were believed to extend to mice, with some herbals recommending scraps of cloth soaked in lavender oil be left at the back of cupboards and other typical mice entrances.

Less well-known is tansy, whose flowers and leaves can be dried and rubbed and then put into similar bags. Horse chestnuts are another traditional moth repellent: put them in the wardrobe and renew them every autumn. Plant lore also ascribes to them the power to repel mice and even spiders.

Plants from the bedstraw family have a good reputation for repelling moths. Sweet woodruff (*Galium odoratum*) is quite odorless until cut and dried, when it develops the heavenly scent of new-mown hay, due to its coumarin content—an aromatic crystalline compound. Lady's bedstraw (*G. verum*) smells similarly sweet when dry, and was once used with straw to stuff mattresses. Unlike sweet woodruff, however, its flowers are scented and smell deliciously of honey.

REPELLENTS TO RUB IN

Dried tansy leaves rubbed into a dog's fur will give the animal some protection against fleas. Dried and rubbed leaves of santolina, southernwood, sage, and mint can be sprinkled on carpets to drive out carpet beetles

LEFT AND BELOW RIGHT: LAVENDER IS AN INCREDIBLY USEFUL PLANT AROUND THE HOUSE. SEWN INTO SACHETS AND LAID AMONGST CLOTHES, THE DRIED FLOWERS NOT ONLY SCENT THEM BUT DETER MOTHS TOO. LAVENDER OIL IS USED TO PERFUME BEESWAX POLISH, WHILE THE FLOWERS ARE A FAVORITE INGREDIENT OF POTPOURRI.

ABOVE RIGHT: AS WELL AS BEING AN IMPORTANT CULINARY HERB, BUNCHES OF MINT LEAVES CAN HELP TO KEEP FLIES OUT OF THE KITCHEN.

Labeling Plants

In his book *The English Flower Garden*, published in 1883, William Robinson wrote, "Do not pay too much attention to labeling; if a plant is not worth knowing, it is not worth growing." He had a point—labeling well-established trees and shrubs can look rather municipal—but there are other situations where labels can be vital.

If you've taken a batch of cuttings, one plantlet can look much like another until they begin to grow, especially if you are preparing cuttings from different varieties of one species—fuchsias, for example. This is even more true of hardwood cuttings, which are just so many twigs in the ground until they take. Simple plastic labels with a marker pen will sort them out.

When planting spring bulbs, unless you put them all in at once, there is every danger of digging up carefully planted daffodils when you come to plant the tulips. Labels will prevent this irritating waste of effort. Use robust labels on fairly long wooden stakes that cats won't scratch up or birds peck aside.

Seeds and herbs

The traditional way to mark rows of seeds—simply piercing the empty seed packet with a twig and pushing this into the end of the row as a temporary marker until the seeds spring up—really can't be improved upon. In the herb garden, similar-looking but different varieties of thyme are worth distinguishing, as are closely related herbs like coriander and chervil. In this case, permanent ornamental markers will look attractive; nostalgic "heritage" mail order catalogs often have punched zinc or verdigris copper labels to push into the soil, while some potters make terra-cotta versions incised with names of herbs.

Nursery labels

Trees and shrubs often come with labels fastened to a branch or stem. If you decide to leave these in place because the name is particularly difficult or visitors' inquiries get tedious—or you simply don't trust your memory—then check the label regularly, as it can cut into the bark as the tree grows. It may be safer to remove it and paste it into your garden logbook (see page 123) for reference.

OPPOSITE: A CLUTCH OF ANTIQUE LABELS THAT RECORD THE SENTIMENTS BEHIND A PLANTING AND THE DATE—AN IDEA THAT COULD BE COPIED FOR A MORE HOMEY GARDEN.

ZINC LABELS

A tip from the nineteenth century, given in an issue of The Gardener's Monthly, *published in 1872, advised oxidizing zinc labels before using them. This involved leaving the labels in water for a day or two. Plant names were then written on using an ordinary lead pencil and it was claimed that, even 12 years later, they still read as easily as when they were first written.*

Latin Names

On a purely practical note, plants' Latin names avoid a great deal of confusion. Those with similar common names are sometimes quite different and it can be annoying to think you've bought one species and realize you've ended up with another. Take quince, for example: the edible quince is *Cydonia oblonga*—a slow-growing tree ultimately 10 feet tall, while the Japanese quince, a small spring-flowering garden shrub, is *Chaenomeles japonica*.

Classifying plants

The system of classification for both plants and animals was developed by the Swedish botanist Linnaeus in the mid-eighteenth century. Latin names generally come in two parts. The first word, known as the generic name, refers to the genus—a group of closely related plants—and is usually a noun of some sort. The second part of the name acts as an adjective, defining each individual species within a genus and containing valuable information about the plant. Where no suitable Latin adjectives existed, Greek words were often Latinized and pressed into service.

When the full Latin names of plants are used and a genus is referred to more than once, the genus is usually abbreviated after the first reference, as in *Viburnum opulus* and *V. plicatum*. Sometimes the generic name is used alone, to refer to the whole genus; for example, *Tagetes spp.* means species of *Tagetes* (marigolds). In many cases the generic name has also become the common name, as for example dianthus and rhododendron.

Many species names indicate the plant's country of origin: *californicus* is obvious; *anatolicus*, refers to the region of Anatolia in Turkey. Others are a useful guide to color: azureus means sky blue; *flava* is yellow; and *alba*, white. Chrysos is golden, from the Greek; and, even more specifically, *chrysocarpos* is a plant bearing golden fruit and *chrysophyllus* one that is golden-leaved.

ANCIENT ORIGINS
....

Greek mythology has supplied an enormous number of plant names. The genus Narcissus refers to the vain Greek youth who fell in love with his own reflection in a pool and drowned as a result. The original generic name for the bluebell, Endymion (now reclassified less romantically as Hyacinthoides), refers to a shepherd boy beloved of Selene, the Greek goddess of the moon. So that she might caress him perpetually, she cast a spell so that he slept for ever. Helios, the Greek god of the sun, gave his name to sunflowers, the genus Helianthus, which always turn their flowers to the sun (anthos is Greek for flower).

ANNUAL SUNFLOWERS GERMINATE, GROW, FLOWER, PRODUCE SEED, AND DIE ALL IN THE SPACE OF A YEAR, HENCE THEIR LATIN NAME *HELIANTHUS ANNUUS.* CULTIVARS INCLUDE 'RUSSIAN GIANT,' 'TEDDY BEAR,' AND 'VELVET QUEEN.'

History lessons

Learning a few key words can unlock a whole history lesson in a single plant name. For example, the genus *Fuchsia* was named after Leonhard Fuchs, a seventeenth-century German botanist, while any Latin name with *banksia* in it refers to the great English plant-hunter Sir Joseph Banks, who accompanied Captain Cook on his epic voyage around the world in the *Endeavor*. *Magnolia soulangeana*, one of the most popular garden species of magnolia, has immortalized the memory of Monsieur Etienne Soulange-Bodin, who was tutor to Empress Josephine's children and whose garden just happened to produce a brand-new cross between two already known magnolia species.

Easy and not so easy

Some Latin names are obvious: no one will have trouble translating *fragrans* (fragrant), *giganteus* (gigantic), *grandis* (big, showy), or *gracilis* (graceful). Others provide valuable clues to a plant's height and habitat: *repens* means low-growing; *oceanicus* indicates a seaside plant; *flore pleno* can mean many flowers. More obscure but no less poetic are *flos-cuculi*—flowering when the cuckoo sings—and *mellifera* or honey-bearing.

Finally, some plants are further defined by an additional Latin variety name that indicates a naturally occurring variation (for example, *Digitalis purpurea albiflora*—the white foxglove); by a cultivar name, in English, that means it is a cultivated variety developed by a plant breeder (for example, *Geranium pratense* 'Mrs. Kendall Clarke'); or by a multiplication sign that attests to a hybrid between two species.

By becoming familiar with a few key Latin names, you can become privy to a true gardening language, an esperanto for passionate gardeners that instantly weeds out the less serious plant lovers.

The Language of Flowers

Flowers have had symbolic associations for centuries. Virginal white madonna lilies have long been linked with the Virgin Mary, while red roses have been an enduring symbol of love for almost as long. But it was not until the nineteenth century that a French writer published a complete "code" of the significance of different flowers. She explained how feelings and ideas could be expressed by combinations of flowers, leaves, grasses, and herbs. This was seized upon with delight by the Victorians with their enthusiasm for sublimating emotion and desire, and it became a language of subterfuge and passion.

The first version

Charlotte de la Tour's *Le Langage des Fleurs* was published in Paris in 1818 and provoked a host of translations and subsequent works. The existence of differing meanings and translations made sending sentiments by posy open to misunderstanding and confusion unless both parties had read the same book.

Many plants already had well-established meanings in British tradition and folklore, so these had to be accommodated in British versions. For example, in de La Tour's book, rosemary is said to mean "your presence revives me," but in England this herb had long been associated with remembrance, as in Shakespeare's *Hamlet*: "There's rosemary, that's for remembrance; pray, love, remember."

Some meanings explained

Many meanings are logical and easy to trace. Bluebells signify constancy as they continue to flourish despite being picked and trampled. Snowdrops represent hope, because they flower in late winter and remind us of the coming spring. Opium poppies symbolize sleep because of their narcotic sap. And twisting, climbing honeysuckle indicates the ties of love. Here are some common flowers and their meanings:

Lavender: *Refusal*

Narcissus: *Egotism*

Primrose: *Emerging love*

Lily of the valley: *Friendship*

Christmas rose: *Anxiety*

Sweet william: *Fun*

Tansy: *Rejection*

Peony: *Contrition*

Oak leaves: *Take courage*

Pimpernel: *Let's meet*

Orchid: *Luxury*

Ivy: *Faithfulness*

HIDDEN MEANINGS

It was not just the type of flower that meant something in the Language of Flowers. Further significance could be inferred from how a posy was tied and how the flowers within it were arranged—any flower included upside down indicated that its meaning should be reversed, so that a violet, usually a symbol of modesty, could come to mean conceit or arrogance.

IN THIS MIXED GARDEN BOUQUET, THE FLOWERS WERE PICKED FOR THEIR LOOKS ALONE, BUT THEIR MEANINGS CONVEY CONFLICT—ROSES SIGNIFY LOVE, BUT THE STEMS OF SNAPDRAGONS TUCKED UNDERNEATH INDICATE THE VERY OPPOSITE.

Keeping a Garden Logbook

A garden logbook can take its place alongside the most essential tools, and if kept up to date and annotated with honesty, it is guaranteed to improve your success rate with growing flowers and vegetables as the years go by.

Different layouts and styles of logbook-keeping will appeal to gardeners whose priorities are different. Vegetable growers will appreciate quite a scholarly diary with pages marked into columns to record sowing dates, weather conditions, maybe even soil temperatures. Pages of graph paper will be useful for drawing up a plan of the vegetable garden and marking on rows of vegetables.

If you have the time, rough sketches made on the back of an envelope can be transferred to the journal proper. Or, if that seems like a waste of effort, the best thing to do is invest in a tough traveler's notebook, the sort with waterproof covers, plus a no-run waterproof pen. There is much to be said for a characterful logbook with battered edges, mud-splashed pages, and the odd squashed blackfly. Equally, a pristine journal written from the relative comfort of the kitchen table is just as useful and can be left lying around on the coffee table rather than being relegated to the shed. Look back at it on dark winter nights and wonder. You are writing the personal history of your garden.

Sketchbooks and scrapbooks

Those of more romantic and artistic bent will prefer something more akin to a sketchbook, where flowers can be drawn and colors noted, color schemes can be plotted and scents compared. Even so, it is vital to date your notes and sketches, which will be rendered meaningless if you can't put them into context.

By choosing a fairly large book, it's possible to compile a combination of scrapbook and gardener's log. Whenever you read an interesting piece of research or a snippet on an unusual plant, cut it out right away and paste it in, to create your own reference book and "wish list" of plants.

HIGH-TECH PLANNING

New technology can make life easier. Absent-minded gardeners could try carrying tape recorders as they walk around their plots. As soon as an idea occurs it can be recorded immediately, to be transcribed and acted on later. Most computer software packages include a facility for drawing, and though this is not the easiest skill to master, it can be useful for drawing up crop rotation plans involving symbols and straight lines. You can also buy specific software for garden design.

LEFT: FILLING A LOG BOOK WITH SKETCHES, PAINTINGS, PRESSED FLOWERS, AND OTHER TOKENS CREATES A UNIQUE GARDENING RECORD THAT WILL ONE DAY BECOME AN HEIRLOOM TO PASS DOWN THROUGH THE FAMILY.

BELOW: A JOBBING NOTEBOOK THAT GOES EVERYWHERE THE GARDENER DOES IS A MINE OF MUD-SPLATTERED INFORMATION.

Useful addresses

**This listing contains internet-accessible businesses that may be able to supply some of the items used in this book. However, inclusion on this list does not constitute an endorsement of the supplier or their products by the publisher.

American Rose Society
P.O. Box 30,000
Shreveport, LA 71130-0030
(318) 938-5402
www.ars.org

Arbor Day Foundation
100 Arbor Ave.
Nebraska City, NE
1-888-448-7337
www.arborday.org

Better Homes & Gardens
Gardening Guide
www.bhglive.com/gardening

Burpee Seeds
800-333-5808
www.burpee.com

The Centre for Alternative Technology, UK
Machynlleth, Powys SY20 9AZ
Tel: (01654) 702400
www.cat.org.uk
Research center dedicated to green living. Good leaflets available on different methods of making compost.

Cook's Garden
P.O. Box 5010
Hodges, SC 29653-5010
800-457-9703
www.cooksgarden.com

The Cottage Garden Society
244 Edleston Road
Crewe, Cheshire CW2 7EJ, UK
Tel: (01270) 250776
www.alfresco.demon.co.uk/cgs/index.html
An informal society set up with the aim of sharing knowledge of old-fashioned plants and traditional cottage gardens.

Farmer's Almanac
Yankee Magazine
P.O. Box 520
Dublin, NH 03444-0520
(603) 563-8111
www.almanac.com

Garden on-line magazine
www.garden.com

Garden Club
www.gardenclub.net

Garden Escape
www.garden.com

Garden Gate Magazine
2200 Grand Ave.
Des Moines, IA 50312
1-800-341-4769
wwwgardengatemagazine.com

The Garden Helper
www.thegardenhelper.com

The Hardy Plant Society
Little Orchard, Great
Comberton, UK
Pershore, Hereford WR10 3DP
Tel: (01386) 710317
www.hardy-plant.org.uk
A society dedicated to conserving older, rarer, and more unusual plants, and making them more widely available to gardeners everywhere.

Henry Doubleday Research Association, UK
Ryton Gardens, Ryton-on-Dunsmore, Coventry CV8 3LG
Tel: (01203) 303517
www.hdra.org.uk
The national center for organic gardening—members are kept up to date with magazines and newsletters. Demonstration gardens on site include a rose garden, meadow garden, vegetable plots and composting areas. Organic seed sold by mail order; free catalog.

Herb Specialists, Canada
Goodwood, Ontario L0C 1A0
(905) 640-6677
www.richters.com

Historical Gardens
The Barn at 189 Cordaville Rd
Southborough, MA 01772-1815
www.traditionalgardening.com

Home & Garden Television
www.hgtv.com

The Internet Garden
www.internetgarden.co.uk

Johnny's Selected Seeds
Foss Hill Road
Albion, ME 04190
Tel. (207) 437-4395
www.johnnyseeds.com

Labelplant, UK
Wroxham Road, Poole
Dorset BH12 1NJ
Plant labels by mail order, including aluminum, copper, and write-on plastic. Send 1st class stamp for catalog.

Logee's Greenhouse
141 North St.
Danielson, CT 06239-1939
1-888-330-8038
www.logees.com

The Milliput Company, UK
Unit 8, The Marian, Dolgellau
Mid Wales LL40 1UU
Tel: (01341) 422562
www.milliput.com
Manufacturers of Milliput epoxy putty for repairing terracotta pots, available by mail order.

National Gardening Assn.
180 Flynn Ave.
Burlington, VT 05401
(802) 863-1308
www.garden.org

Peter Beale's Roses, UK
London Road, Attleborough
Norfolk NR17 1AY
Tel: (01953) 454707
*More than 1,100 varieties of rose
available by mail order.*

The Recycle Works, UK
The Rookery, Chatburn
Clitheroe BB7 4AW
Tel: (01200) 440600.
www.recycleworks.co.uk
*Self-assembly wooden compost
bins that need no nails or screws,
plus wormeries and leaf-mold
composters, available by mail
order.*

Ponds, Pools & Fountains
5508 Elmwod Ave, Suite 411
Indianapolis, IN 46203
1-800-651-0002
www.ppfc.com

The Secret Garden Shop
www.secretgardenshop.com

Southern Gardening
P.O. Box 2488
Gainesville, FL 32602-2488
www.southerngardening.com

Split Rock Ponds
Monmouth County, NJ
1-800-352-7826
www.walnet.com/splitrock/

Smith & Hawken
Locations nationally
1-800-940-1170
www.smith-hawken.com

Two Wests & Elliot, UK
Unit 4, Carrwood Road
Sheepbridge Industrial Estate
Chesterfield
Derbyshire S41 9RH
Tel: (01246) 451077
*Mail order catalog specializing
in greenhouse and conservatory
equipment, plus a useful source of
diverter kits for household
downpipes, seep hoses, and
aluminum plant labels.*

**United States Department of
Agriculture** (USDA)
14th & Independence Ave SW
Washington, D.C. 20250
(202) 720-2791
www.usda.gov/news/garden

Van Ness Water Garden
2460 N. Euclid Ave.
Upland, CA 91784-1199
1-800-205-2425
www.vnwg.com

Virtual Garden
www.vg.com

Wiggly Wigglers, UK
Lower Blakemere Farm
Herefordshire HR2 9PX
Tel: (01981) 500391
www.wigglywigglers.co.uk
*Wormeries and compost bins by
mail order.*

Willow Pond Nursery
P.O. Box 192
Hewlett, NY
(516) 374-2522
www.willowpondnursery.com

World Seed
300 Morning Drive
Bakersfield, CA 93306
www.worldseed.com

Yard Care
www.yardcare.com

index

Page numbers in italics refer to photographs.

A
abutilons 39
acanthus 21
African marigolds 114
Agrostis species 52
allelopathy 110–11
Allium sphaerocephalon 97
angelica (*Angelica archangelica*) *55*, 112
ant deterrents 114
aphids/aphid-eaters 109, 110, 112–13
apples:
  drying 81
  storing 80–1, *81*
aquilegias 72
artemesia 21
arum lilies (*Zantedeschia aethiopica*) 103
asparagus 108
asplenium 76
B
Banks, Sir Joseph 119
bark chippings 33, 95
basil 106, 111
bay leaves 114
beans and peas (legumes) *24–5*, 34
  companion planting 106, 108, 112–13
bedstraw family 115
bells of Ireland (*Moluccella laevis*) 54, *78*, 79
benches 11, 14
bindweed (*Convolvulus arvensis*) 22, 27, 47
blackberries 63
blackfly 112
bluebells (*Hyacinthoides non-scripta*) 76, 118, 120
bog plants 103
box boundaries *24–5*
brandling worms 28
brooklime (*Veronica beccabunga*) 103
broom (*Cytisus* spp.) 21, 97
bugle (*Ajuga reptans*) 47
bulbs, spring 76, 77, *99*
  for fragrance 70
  labeling 116
  in lawns 51
C
cabbage family (brassicas) 34, *35*
  companion planting 106, 108
  storing 82
cabbage root fly 108
cabbage roses (*Rosa x centifolia*) 69
cabbage white caterpillars 106, 112

California poppies (*Eschscholzia californica*) 112
camellias 21, 25, 42, 86
camomile 14
  Chamaemelum nobile 'Treneague' 52
campanulas 72
Canary creeper (*Tropaeolum peregrinum*) 10
candelabra primulas 103
candytuft (*Iberis*) 112
caper spurge (*Euphorbia lathyris*) 51
capillary systems 93
carpet mulches 32
carrot fly 106, *107*
caterpillar control 106, 112
catkins 112, *112*
catmint (*Nepeta* spp.) 110
chalky soil 21
chicken manure, treating 31
Chilean glory vine (*Eccremocarpus scaber*) 10
chimney pots 42
China asters 54
chives *24–5*
Christmas rose 120
chrysanthemums 51
cinquefoil (*Potentilla reptans*) 47
clamps and silos 83
clarkia 54
clay soil 18, 22
clematis 21, *38–9*, 51
click beetles 32
  larvae *see* wireworms
climbing plants 10, 69
cloches 36, *61*
club root disease 34, *35*
cockroaches 114
cold frames 66
cold snaps 58
comfrey (*Symphytum grandiflorum*) 47, 98
companion planting 11, *106–7*, 106–11, *109, 110, 111, 113*
  see also allelopathy
compost 26, 27, 28
  heaps and containers 28
  and soil structure 18
containers 42–3, *42–3, 44*, 45
  frost protection 60
convolvulus (*Convulvulus tricolor*) 112
cosmos 54
cottage garden annuals 54
couch grass (*Elymus repens*) 22, 27, 32, 47
coumarin 52, 115
cow parsley (*Anthriscus sylvestris*) 112
creeping buttercup (*Ranunculus repens*) 27, 32, 47
creeping thistle (*Cirsium arvense*) 47
crocuses 52, 76
crop rotation 30, 34, *35*

cup-and-saucer vine (*Cobaea scandens*) 10
cutting garden 54, *55*
cuttings 38–9, *38–9*
  labeling 116
D
daffodils 52, 54
dahlias 51, 54
  sealing stems 54
daisy grubber 13
dandelions 51, 58
Daphne mesereum and *odora* 70
deckchairs 15
deep-water plants 103
delphiniums 54, *55*, 72–3, *74, 75*
digging 22, *22*
  wet soil 22
diseases:
  preventing 34
  rose beds 110
dock (*Rumex obtusifolium*) 22, 47
dog's-tooth violets (*Erythronium dens-canis*) 76
drought-affected sites 97
drought-resistant plants 74, *96*, 96, *97*, 97
  and soil type 21
dry shade 76
drying flowers *78*, 78–9
  using silica gel 79
  what to grow 78–9
E
earwig traps 51
eggplant 65
elder (*Sambucus*) 38, 114
Encarsia formosa 66
eryngium 112
evening primrose (*Oenothera biennis*) 69
evening scents 69
'everlasting flowers' *78*, 78
F
fennel (*Foeniculum vulgare*) 112
ferns 76, 103
fertilizers:
  liquid 27, 98, *98*, 99
    high-potash 98
  worm-cast 28
Festuca species 52
figwort (*Scrophularia auriculata*) 103
flea protection *115*
flies, deterring 114
flower garden:
  raised beds 24
  tools 13
  weed suppressers 47
flowering currant (*Ribes*) 38
flowering plants:
  extending the season 63, 112
  scented *68*, 69–70, *71*

underfoot 70
  and soil type 21
  when to cut 54
    sealing stems 54
  see also cutting garden; drying flowers
flowering tobacco (*Nicotiana sylvestris*) 69
fly repellents 114, *115*
foliar feeds 98, *99*
forget-me-nots (*Myosotis*) 72
forsythia 21, 38
foxgloves (*Digitalis purpurea*) 54, 72, 72
  companion planting 110, *111*
  D. p. albiflora 119
foxtail millet (*Setaria italica*) 79
French marigolds (*Tagetes patula*) 14, 106
frost/frost protection 58, 59, 60, 61, *61*, 63
  preparing for late frosts 60
  preventing pockets 63
fruit trees 74
  frost protection 60
  see also apples; pears
Fuchs, Leonhard 119
fuchsias 39, 45, 119
furniture *11*, 14–15, *14–15*
  junk-shop finds 14, *14*
  painting 14
G
garden logbook 116, *122, 123*
garlic, companion planting 110, *111*
  see also under Allium spp.
geraniums 44. 47. 64–5, 76
  ivy-leaved 45
  scented 70
  G. pratense 'Mrs. Kendall Clarke' 119
globe thistles (*Echinops*) *55*, 79
globeflowers (*Trollius* spp.) 103
godetia 54
goldenrod (*Solidago* spp.) 79
grasses:
  lawn species 52
  ornamental 79, 103
greasebands 66
green manure 22, 30, 47
greenhouses 64–5, *65*–6, 67
  biological warfare 66
  companion planting 108
  frost-free 61, 65
  spring cleaning 66
ground elder (*Aegopodium podagraria*) 27, 47
ground ivy (*Glechoma hederacea*) 47
ground preparation 22, *22*, 54
  cutting garden 54
gypsophila (baby's breath) 79
H
hammocks 14

hanging baskets 45
hare's-tail grass (*Lagurus ovatus*) 79
hawthorn 21
heaters, greenhouse 65
  mini homemade 61
heathers 21
hedges 63
  pruning 48
helichrysum 45
hellebores 21, 72, 73
herb Robert (*Geranium robertianum*)
    47
herbs *24–5*, 43
  along pathways 70
  companion planting 106, *106–7*
  labeling 116
  as lawn 52
  see also individual herbs
hoes 47
hollyhocks 54, 113
honesty (*Lunaria annua*) 72, 79
honeysuckle *38–9*, 71
  winter (*Lonicera fragrantissima*) 70
horse chestnuts 115
horseradish 108
hose pipes 92
  irrigation by 32
hostas 76, 103
hot bed, making 66
houseleek (*Sempervivum*) 97
hoverflies 110, *112–13*
  larvae 112
hydrangeas 39, 60, 76
hyssop 106

I
ice 58
  on ponds 100
'immortelles' 78
incense rose (*Rosa primula*) 69
insect-attracting plants 110, *112*,
    112–13, *113*
insect-repelling plants *114–15*, *114–15*
irises 103
  dividing 39
  miniature (*I. reticulata*) 70
  wild (*I. versicolor/I. pseudoacorus*) 103
irrigation *92–3*, *93*
ivy 45, 47, 112, 120

J
Jerusalem artichoke windbreak 63
Jerusalem sage (*Phlomis fruticosa*) 97

L
labeling plants 116, *117*
ladybugs 47, 113
lady's bedstraw (*Galium verum*) 115
lamb's ears (*Stachys lanata*) 97
language of flowers 120
  hidden meanings 120, *121*
larkspur (*Consolida ambigua*) 54, 79
lavender (*Lavandula* spp.) 21, *43*, 70,
    96, 97, 114, *114*, *115*, 120

lawnmowers 52
lawns 52, *53*
  alternative 51
  cuttings in compost 26
  mowing during dry spells 95
  planting in 51
  watering 90
leaf mould 25, 28, *28–9*
leek flowers *110*
ligularias 103
lilac 21, 69
lilies *64–5*, 70
  for shade 76
  Lilium martagon 76
lily of the valley 111, 120
Linnaeus 118
lobelias 45, 103
love-in-a-mist (*Nigella damascena*) 54,
    72, 79
lungwort (*Pulmonaria officinalis*) 76
lupins 110
lychnis spp. 21, 47
  L. coronaria 72

M
Magnolia soulangeana 119
mahonia 70
manure 30, 66
  improving soil structure 18, 19, 22
  liquid 66, 98
  see also chicken manure; green
    manure
marginal plants 103
marsh marigold (*Caltha palustris*)
    103
marvel of Peru (*Mirabilis jalapa*) 69
meadow grass (*Poa* spp.) 52
mealy cabbage aphid 108
Michaelmas daisies 112
mignonette (*Reseda lutea*) 70, 110,
    111
mint 106, 114, 115, *115*
moles 51
moth/mouse repellents *114–15*
mulches/mulching 32, 33
  manmade 94
  permanent 33
  to retain moisture 94, *95*
  under roses 110

N
Narcissus 118, 120
narrow-leaved plants 97
nasturtiums 21
  as pest control 108
nettles 47, 98, 113
night-scented stock (*Matthiola
    longipetala*) 69
nitrogen-fixing plants 34, 110
  see also green manure
nursery labels 116

O
oak leaves 120

onions:
  companion planting 106, *107*
  stringing 83
orchid 120
organic manure 30

P
pansies 72
parsley 110
pears, storing 81
pennyroyal (*Mentha pulegium*) 14
peony 120
peppers (*Capsicum*) 106
periwinkle (*Vinca major*) 76
pest control 51, 112
  companion planting and 106, 108
  in the kitchen 114
  mulching and 32
  natural/biological 66, 100
  see also insect-repelling plants
phacelia 112
philadelphus 38
phlox 54, 55, 103
phormiums 97
pH value 21
pickerel weed (*Pontederia cordata*)
    103
pieris 42
pinks 55
plant antipathy *see* allelopathy
plant classification *118–19*
  Latin names 118
plant toxins *see* allelopathy
plastic sheeting (black) 32, 33, 47
plume poppy (*Macleaya microcarpa*)
    89
poached-egg flower (*Limnanthes
    douglasii*) 110, *112–13*
pocket knife 13
pollination 112, 113
Polypodium vulgare 76
ponds 100
poor man's weather glass 58
poppies 120
  sealing stems 54
  seedheads 79
porous piping 92
potager *24–5*
potatoes 32, 34
  as weed suppressors 47
  companion planting 106, 108, 111
  storing 82
potentillas 97
pots 40
  advantages of plastic 40
  watering 90
  see also terra cotta
potting bench 10
pressing flowers 78
primroses (*Primula vulgaris*) 70, 76,
    120
pruning 48, *49*

pruning saw 48

Q
quaking grass (*Briza* spp.) 79
quince:
  edible (*Cydonia oblonga*) 118
  Japanese (*Chaenomeles japonica*) 118

R
rain, predicting 58
raised beds *24–5*, *24–5*
  shady 76
red campion (*Silene diocia*) 47
rhododendrons and azaleas 21, 25,
    42, 86
  companion planting 110
Robinson, William 116
root crops, storing *82–3*
rosemary (*Rosmarinus* spp.) 21, *43*,
    70, 97, 106, 120
roses 21, 69, 71, 74, 120, *121*
  companion planting 110, *111*
  'Constance Spry' *71*
  propagating 39
  pruning 48, *49*
  replanting disease 110
rotavators 22
rue 111
rushes 103
ryegrass (*Lolium perenne*) 52

S
sage 43, 106, *106–7*
sandy soil 18
santolina 115
scarlet pimpernel (*Anagallis arvensis*)
    58, 120
scent warfare 106
scrapbooks 123
seating *11*, 14, *14*, *15*, 70
seaweed mulch 33
secateurs 48
  cleaning 13
sedum 97
seed sowing 36
  direct 36, *36–7*
  indoors 36, 65
  labeling after 116
  treating tough seeds 37
seedheads, dried 79
seeds 72
  collecting *72–3*
  labeling and storing 73
seed trays 4
self-seeding plants 72, *72*, 73
shade, gardening in 74, 76, *77*
Shasta daisies (*Leucanthemum x
    superba*) 112
sheds 10, *11*
  painting or disguising 10
shredded bark 33
shredders 33
shrubs:
  in containers 42

for dappled shade 76
pruning 48
taking cuttings 38–9, *38–9*
silver and gray plants *43*, 97
sketchbooks 123
slug/snail damage *50*, 51
snakeshead fritillaries (*Fritallaria meleagris*) 52
snapdragons *121*
snow 58
snowdrops (*Galanthus* spp.) 52, 70, 76, 77, 120
soil 18
   determining type 21
      see also ground preparation; *and individual soil types*
   improving 18, *19*, 30
   raised beds 24, 25
   removing large stones 20
   seed beds 36
soil acidity 21
   maintaining 25
soil-testing kits 21
Soulange-Bodin, Etienne 119
southernwood (*Artemisia abrotanum*) 106, 115
spear thistles 47
specific replant disease 110
spider flower (*Cleome spinosa*) 54, 72
spring:
   bouquets 54
   bulbs 52
   scented plants for 70
sprinkler systems 90, *93*
statice (*Limonium*) 78
storage *11*, *12*
   fruit *80–1*, 81
   hose pipes 92
   pots 41, *41*

seeds 73
vegetables 10, 81, 82–3, *82–3*
strawberry-growing 32, 34
   in planters 45
strawflowers (*Helichrysum bracteatum*) 78, *78*
succulents 97
sun, gardening in 74, *74–5*
sunflowers (*Helianthus*) *74*, 111, 112, 118, *118–19*
sweet briar (*Rosa rubiginosa*) 69
sweet peas 60, 68, 69, 72, 111
sweet rocket (*Hesperis matronalis*) 70, 72
sweet scabius (*Scabiosa atropurpurea*) 54
sweet vernal grass (*Anthoxanthum odoratum*) 52
sweet william 120
sweet woodruff (*Galium odoratum*) 47, 115
sweetcorn 24–5
T
tansy 114, 115, 120
terra cotta:
   aging 40
   storing/repairing 41, *41*
Thalia dealbata 88
thiophenes 106
thyme 14, 52, 70, 106, 110
tiger worms 28
toad lilies (*Tricyrtis*) 76
tomatoes 65, *82*, *108*
   companion planting 108
tools *12*, 13
   improvising 13
   maintenance 13
   minimum required 13
   storing 10

Tour, Charlotte de la 120
tree mallow (*Lavatera arborea*) 38
trellis 63
tulips 54, *99*
turf bench 14
U
umbellifer family 112
V
vegetable garden 74
   companion planting 106–8, *107*, *109*
   raised beds 24–5, *24–5*
   soil maintenance *19*
   tools 13, 47
   windbreaks 63
   see also crop rotation
vegetables 10, 81, 82–3, *82–3*
   suppressing weeds with 47
verbascum 54
Verbena bonariensis 54
W
walnut trees 111
wasps 112, 114
water:
   collecting 86, *86*
   lime-free 86
   recycling household 86
   reducing loss of 32, 94, *95*
water barrows 92
water cure 90
water hawthorn (*Aponogeton distachyos*) 103
water lilies (*Nymphaea* spp.) 101, 102
water violet (*Hottinia palustris*) 103
watering 89–90
   greenhouses 65
   hanging baskets 45
   shock prevention 89
   see also irrigation
watering cans 86, *87*, *91*

water-loving plants *102*, 103
   preventing rampant growth 103
water-retaining granules 45
weather, predicting 58
weather map, personalized 58
weed control 24, 27, 32, 47
   lawns 51
   paths *46*
   with plants 47
   seedbeds 37
weeds 47
   adding to compost bin 26
   rotavating and 22
wheelbarrows *23*, 27
whitefly 106, 108
willow (*Salix*) 38
windbreaks 62–3, *63*
window boxes 45
winter, scented plants for 70
wintersweet (*Chimonanthus* spp.) 70
wireworms 51
witch hazel (*Hamamelis* spp.) 70
wood anemones (*Anemone nemorosa*) 76
wood avens (*Geum urbanum*) 47
worm bins 28
X
Xeranthemum annuum 78
Y
yarrow (*Achillea millefolum*) 112
yellow skunk cabbage (*Lysichiton americanus*) 103

Picture acknowledgments

Caroline Arber: 5, 91
Clive Boursnell: 95
Jean Cazals: 37
Charlie Colmer: 9, 16, 59, 77, 111 (bottom), 112
Melanie Eclare: 29, 39, 75
Craig Fordham: 23, 28, 35, 83, 87, 107, 116
Kate Gadsby: 44, 111 (top), 115 (bottom)
Jane Gifford: 55 (bottom), 109, 110
Georgia Glynn-Smith: 11, 55 (top), 98
Huntley Hedworth: 31
Jacqui Hurst: 12, 22, 41, 74, 78, 80, 93, 97, 99, 123
Tom Leighton: 15, 42
Jill Mead: 96, 114
James Merrell: 33, 49, 68, 108, 115 (top)

Andrew Montgomery: 122
Debbie Patterson: 81
Michael Paul: 84, 88, 89, 101, 102
Clay Perry: 24, 53, 62, 67, 104, 106, 119
Spike Powell: 40, 82, 113
Alex Ramsey: 56, 71
Stephen Robson: 64, 72
William Shaw: 46
Ian Skelton: 19, 20, 27, 50
Pia Tryde: 1, 2, 7, 14, 43, 61, 73, 121

Styling by Ben Kendrick (pages 1, 2, 7, 43, 55 and 61), Hester Page (pages 5 and 9) and Pippa Rimmer (pages 11 and 44).